Just the Job

Just the Job

How Trades got their Names

ALEXANDER TULLOCH

Bodleian Library
UNIVERSITY OF OXFORD

First published in 2020 by the Bodleian Library
Broad Street, Oxford OX1 3BG
www.bodleianshop.co.uk

ISBN 978 1 85124 550 5

Cover design by Dot Little at the Bodleian Library
Designed and typeset in 10½ on 14 Baskerville by illuminati, Grosmont
Printed and bound in China by C&C Offset Printing Co. Ltd
on 120 gsm Chinese Baijin pure woodfree paper

British Library Catalogue in Publishing Data
A CIP record of this publication is available from the British Library

CONTENTS

INTRODUCTION

It is probably something of a cliché, but nonetheless a valid observation, that societies resemble machines. Both societies and machines, if they are to function smoothly and efficiently, rely on moving parts operating independently yet in harmony with each other. A machine has cogs, wheels and pistons, each of which has its own role to play so that the unit as a whole fulfils the function for which it was intended. Society has people and, if it is to function as it should, each member of the workforce is required to fulfil whatever task he or she has been assigned. And in both a machine and society, there is a dynamic interdependence: if a fan belt breaks, the wheel won't turn and the piston will come to an abrupt halt. In simple terms, in most societies, bankers make money, schoolteachers teach children, and office staff carry out their myriad tasks only as long as they can rely on the people who will provide their food, keep the plumbing working, build their houses and organize the transport which will get them to their respective places of work.

Consequently, for reasons of probably little more than practical convenience and easy reference, people have always been identified and defined by the role they fulfil in society. And such definitions survive today as the name tags by which the various occupations are known.

The words we use to define the separate roles we all play in society tend to fall into generally accepted categories. We refer to some of them as 'jobs', some as 'careers' and then there are the 'professions', 'trades' and 'occupations'. And all these terms have distinctive derivations and societal implications, not least because the question of identity is often combined with society's attitudes to how a person earns a living. The dividing lines can be somewhat (not to say *very*) blurred but, generally speaking, manual workers have 'jobs' and are paid a wage; educated people enter the 'professions' and receive a salary; and those who buy and sell goods are defined by their 'trade'. 'Occupation', however, seems to be generically fairly, but not entirely, neutral.

'Job' first entered English in the 1550s (the expression *gobbe of worke* is recorded) meaning a specific task that has to be completed, as opposed to a continuous, extended period of labour. Ultimately, the word is possibly derived from the Irish Gaelic *gob*, meaning 'mouth', so that a 'job' was originally a 'mouthful' (i.e. a small amount) of necessary activity.

In those days, if the manner by which a person fed their family and put a roof over their heads involved travel, they would almost automatically be involved in 'trade'. The word is etymologically related to the verb 'tread', as a 'tradesman' or 'tradeswoman' historically 'trod' around the neighbourhood selling his or her wares or offering services.

During the Middle Ages people who for one reason or another had decided to devote their lives to religion and become a member of a particular religious order would have 'professed' their devotion to their god. A few centuries later the noun 'profession' was retained for those who 'professed' to be skilled in one of the 'higher' occupations (one for which a recognized qualification was required) such as medicine, the law or the church. And the same custom has provided the title by which high-ranking members of a university are known today, 'professors'.

Anybody who follows a 'career' has only been able to do so since the nineteenth century, as previously, beginning in the sixteenth, the word meant either 'a racecourse' or, as a verb, 'to gallop at full speed'. No doubt the first 'careerists' were people who made rapid progress in whatever occupation they chose and might have been spoken about much as we talk now of society's 'high-flyers'.

Roughly speaking, the jobs, trades and occupations contained within this volume divide into three groups: those which existed in the past but which have now disappeared altogether ('gongfarmer', 'pardoner', 'telegraph boy'); those which were known in ancient times and have survived to the present day, even if some are no longer as common as they were ('harbinger', 'currier', 'beadle'); and those which are of recent coinage, reflecting the changing complexion of society in the modern era ('wedding planner', 'best boy', 'cloud architect').

I have also, where relevant, indicated where the trades and jobs of yesteryear survive now as surnames. Some of these are obvious pointers to what family members did for a living in times gone by (Baker, Tanner, Miller), but others have lost their original meanings over the years and are now simply surnames whose origins are forgotten or no longer appreciated (Hayward, Stewart, Barker, Spencer).

It is to be hoped that anyone with an interest in social history will find the following descriptions of the individual occupations illuminating. But I have also introduced an additional dimension by combining the historical descriptions with a brief consideration of the etymologies and derivations behind the headwords themselves. This serves as a reminder that social and linguistic histories frequently go hand in hand.

One of the most noticeable social changes the country, if not the world, has experienced over the last hundred years or so is the breakdown of the barriers between the sexes in the labour market. By the mid-twentieth century, the demands of two world wars, when thousands of men were away from home fighting 'for King and Country', meant that women were required to take on many of the jobs traditionally open only to men. They learned how to operate lathes, drove the buses, became bricklayers, were taught how to repair aeroplanes, qualified as doctors, engineers or mechanics. In other words, they kept the wheels of society turning, both literally and metaphorically, and consequently caused a major rethink about who should do what in the workplace.

The result of this social change is that many of the trades and occupations mentioned in the following pages are now open to men and women alike, whereas at one time they would have been the preserve of either men or women, but not both. Who would have thought, for instance, just a few decades ago that in twenty-first- century Britain the term 'front-line soldier' would one day apply equally to a woman as to a man? And who, furthermore, would have imagined that in 2017 a woman stood just as good a chance of becoming Commissioner of London's Metropolitan Police as any of her male colleagues? Perhaps the Greek philosopher Heraclitus (*c.* 535–*c.* 457 BCE) hit the nail on the head when he said 'everything flows; nothing stands still'.

Admiral

This is now a title enjoyed by the highest-ranking naval officer in most countries of the world, but the derivation of the word is very definitely land-based. It entered English around 1200 as 'amiral', acquired from the French *amirail*, a term borrowed from the Arabic for a Saracen military commander. The original Arabic term *'amīr* (or *emir*) defined the leader of an army but was also applied to non-military rulers such as princes or governors; the derivative verb is *'amara*, 'to command'. It is probably safe to assume that the absorption of this word into European languages had something to do with the Crusades and the contact made between Europeans and Arabian sailors in and around the Mediterranean. Other Arabic words associated with administration and command that found their way into English include *caliph*, 'successor of Muhammad'; *sultan*, 'ruler'; and *wazir*, 'advisor'.

The word 'admiral' was not applied to a naval commander in English until the fifteenth century. This was when another Arabic term, *'amīr al-bahr* (literally 'ruler of the sea'), was borrowed and the first two words were combined to form the word 'amiral'. So the question is, where did the latter 'd' come from? And the answer is: we cannot be absolutely sure but the consensus of opinion among etymologists is that it is by confusion with the similar looking word 'admire', derived from the Latin *admirari*, 'to regard with wonder'. Presumably, few admirals have ever objected to the etymological association.

> Admirals all, for England's sake,
> Honour be yours and fame!
> And honour, as long as the waves shall break,
> To Nelson's peerless name.
>
> SIR HENRY NEWBOLT, 'Admirals All' (1897)

Ambulance driver

The men and women who drive our ambulances play a critical role in society. In the event of an accident in the home or a serious emergency in the community, these doughty saviours of citizens in distress are on the scene as soon as is humanly possible, administering medical attention. If the injuries are slight, the patient is patched up and made comfortable or sent on his or her way. But the more seriously sick and injured, who perhaps cannot walk, are stretchered into the ambulance and taken to the nearest hospital. And this is something of a paradox:

the word itself goes all the way back to the Latin verb *ambulare*, 'to walk', 'to be mobile', but an 'ambulance case' is a person who is too ill to walk and is possibly 'immobile'. The explanation for this apparent contradiction in terms is as follows.

In the seventeenth century the French came up with *hôpital ambulant*, 'mobile hospital', a term which became increasingly popular, so that by the time of the Crimean War (1853–56) it was being used in both a military and a civilian context. It was about this time also that the derivative form 'ambulance' was first recorded.

In 1897 another related term was coined: 'ambulance chaser'. This was (and still is) a derogatory term for predatory lawyers who persuaded people who had been injured through no fault of their own to allow them to act on their behalf when lodging a claim for substantial damages. And, of course, their services command a large fee.

Archer

Archers, or bowmen, have been around for a very long time. Archery, both as a sport and as a means of waging war, was practised by the Ancient Chinese, the Romans, the Greeks and a whole host of other civilizations that have long since been confined to the annals of history. Odysseus, in Homer's *Odyssey* (*c.* eighth century BCE), was a renowned skilful bowman; English archers wrought havoc on the French troops at the battle of Crécy (1346); and the Parthians mastered the art of swivelling in their saddles so that they could fire a 'Parthian shot' at a pursuing enemy. (The Parthian Empire lasted 247–224 CE.)

In England the term 'archer' first made its appearance in the late thirteenth century, a derivative of the Old French *archier*, derived from the Late Latin *arcarius*. And the origin of both these terms was the Latin *arcus*, meaning 'a bow'. Fascinatingly, there is a direct etymological link here with the Greek *arkeuthis*, the Ancient Greeks' term for the tree we know as the juniper, which has strong but flexible branches, the ideal material for any bow maker.

'Arrow' was not common in English until the early fourteenth century, when it finally replaced the Old English *strǣl*, which had been becoming increasingly obsolete since the eleventh century. And the word used in Anglo-Saxon England, *strǣl*, is directly linked to the modern Russian *strelá*, 'arrow', and the verb *strelyát'*, 'to shoot'.

Auditor

Companies, businesses and firms are sometimes required to have 'audits' of their finances conducted in order to make sure that their financial affairs and records are in order. The appointed auditor will check that the money flowing in and out of a firm is being accurately recorded and processed and that all is as it should be, legally speaking. Generally, the auditor will make sure all accounts provide true and fair reflection of how a business is performing.

He or she will frequently sit alone in an office, examining 'the books' in great detail, possibly for lengthy periods without speaking to or hearing from anyone. Consultation with those whose books are being examined might occur only as and when the 'auditor' needs clarification. And this is all rather strange when we look at the derivation of the word.

In the fourteenth century, when accounts were being checked for accuracy and to make sure the correct taxes had been paid to the Crown, almost the whole process was conducted orally. The 'auditor' would listen to the information being provided, perhaps ask a few questions, and then make a final written statement to the effect that all was in order (or not).

The word *auditour* was adopted in the 1300s from the Old French *auditeur*, a word that could trace its origins back to the Latin verb *audire*, 'to listen' or 'to hear'. In

Ancient Rome the derivative noun *auditor* meant basically anyone who 'listened', and it eventually acquired the wider meaning of 'pupil' or 'scholar'. In other words, in this context, an *auditor* was a student willing to 'listen' to what somebody else had to say.

And we can assume that such 'listeners' were prepared to do as they were told or 'obey' any instructions given, as 'obey' is from the Latin *obedire*, a compound verb based on the prefix *ob*, 'to', and *audire*, 'to listen'. 'Obeying', therefore, basically means 'listening to' instructions and acting on them, which is what the medieval auditors did.

[I]t is the disease of not listening, the malady of not marking, that I am troubled withal.

WILLIAM SHAKESPEARE, *2 Henry IV* (1597?), I.2

Bailiff

Most people now associate this term with the person who turns up on the doorstep and demands that outstanding debts be settled otherwise he will remove goods to the value of the sum involved. But in other parts of the world a bailiff has very different functions. In America a bailiff is a court official who looks after and keeps an eye on the prisoners, and in the Channel Islands (Guernsey and Jersey) the chief justice with important administrative and ceremonial duties to perform. In Scotland he is known as a 'bailie' and performs the duties associated elsewhere in the UK with a magistrate.

But whatever the function of a 'bailiff' the derivation of the term is the same. The word entered English in the fourteenth century, borrowed from the Old French *baillif*, itself related to the Latin *baiulus*, meaning 'carrier' or 'porter', linked to the verb *baiulare*, 'to bear a burden', 'to carry a heavy load'. In the same century the basic idea of the word acquired a more metaphorical hue, so that the term 'bailiff' was applied to appointees required to 'bear the heavy responsibilities of office', hence he could be a landlord's steward or represent the monarch as the chief officer of a 'hundred' (an administrative district in England in the Middle Ages).

Another related word is the Old French *bail*, 'control', which we still use today when a person charged with an offence is released 'on bail', meaning that they are free to leave court but that their freedom is strictly 'controlled'.

In the seventeenth century, yet another official made his appearance: the 'bum bailiff'; there are two explanations as to how this representative of the law came to be so called. The first is that he would chase miscreants relentlessly, always hot on their heels and close to their 'bums '; the other suggestion involves the same proximity of pursuit, but emphasizes his habit of grabbing hold of his prey by the seat of his pants.

The office of bailiff has also given us the not uncommon surname 'Bailey'.

Baker

Bakers have been baking bread of one sort or another since the dawn of time; the linguistic roots of the English term stretch back over the millennia as far as Ancient Greece and even earlier. The Ancient Greek verb *phōgein* meant 'to roast' and is etymologically related to the Old High German *bahhan* and the Old English *bacan*, verbs which produced the Old English term for the man we now refer to as a 'baker', *bæcere*. The female equivalent, a woman baker, was a *bekstere*, which eventually gave us the surname Baxter.

But there is also a very odd cognate here. The Indo-European root that produced all of these words (*bheg*) also produced the word 'bath'. The explanation is quite straightforward, if a little surprising; from an etymological point of view, 'bath' was originally associated with heating, not with immersion. The English spa town of Bath took its name from the 'hot' springs in the area, not the springs themselves.

In the 1590s the expression 'a baker's dozen' was heard for the first time in England, originally denoting thirteen loaves instead of twelve. There have been several explanations for this curious feature of the language, but the one now considered the most likely is as follows.

In 1266 King Henry III promulgated the Assize of Bread and Ale, an administrative body responsible for ensuring that the various rules and regulations affecting bakers and brewers were strictly adhered to. Specifically, bakers had to make sure their product met certain standards of weight and quality; if they failed to do so they were liable to be heavily fined (and, according to some sources, beaten). They probably had to trust to skill and a certain amount of luck over quality, but in order to make up for any shortfall in the overall weight they added an extra loaf, referred to as the 'vantage loaf'.

The threat of being punished was obviously still present three hundred years after Henry's ruling.

> Cast thy bread upon the waters; for thou shalt find it
> after many days.
>
> Ecclesiastes 11.1

Banker

We can't be absolutely sure when the first bankers appeared on the scene, but we do know that they have been around for a very long time. Ancient civilizations in the Middle East, Greece and Rome, and even as far afield as China, had some form of monetary regulation and control. It is generally thought, however, that banking as we understand the word today can trace its origins back to medieval Italy. Cities such as Florence, Venice and Genoa, at the time of the Renaissance witnessed a burgeoning of financial activity which we recognize today as modern (if embryonic) banking. Indeed, possibly the oldest bank in the world (which has been offering financial services continuously since 1472) is the Banca Monte dei Paschi di Siena in the northern Italian city of Siena.

The word 'banker' entered English in the 1530s, although it designated a professional whom we would associate more with a moneylender or usurer; the modern banker probably arrived with the first 'banks' (establishments designed for the safe custody and protection of our money) in the seventeenth century.

If we return to Florence and Venice we discover where the word 'bank' originally came from. It entered English from the French *banque*, derived from the Italian *banca* (also closely related to the English 'bench'), originally the table on which the medieval moneylenders counted out their coins and kept records of how much had been lent to whom and at what rate of interest. There is, however, another connection with today's world of finance. If one of the early Italian bankers went out of business, he was required to destroy his *banca* as a sign that he was no longer able to trade. And the Italian for a 'smashed table' is *banca rotta*, from which we derive the word 'bankrupt'.

But there is yet another link. The medieval Italian banker, standing at his *banca* all day, would have to sustain himself with snacks or light meals with perhaps the odd glass of wine. He would no doubt have sat on his *banchetto* ('little bench') while he enjoyed his modest but sustaining snack. And this light bite evolved in meaning into a lavish meal or 'banquet' some time after it entered English in the fifteenth century.

Many words used in everyday English are Italian in origin. Here are a few, with their literal meanings:

Influenza	influence
Piano(forte)	soft(hard)
Opera	work
Replica	repeat performance
Terracotta	baked earth
Al dente	to the tooth
Al fresco	in the fresh air
Ciabatta	slipper (and bread shaped like one)
Espresso	expressed (i.e. squeezed out)
Minestrone	soup
Spaghetti	little strings
Vermicelli	little worms
Jeans	from Genoa
Umbrella	little shade

Barber

The distinctions have become somewhat blurred of late, but traditionally men went to the barber to have their hair cut and women went to the hairdresser. The reason for the distinction is historical and linguistic.

The term 'barber' entered English in the fourteenth century, borrowed from Anglo-Norman *barbour*, from the Old French *barbier* and ultimately from the Latin *barba*, meaning 'beard'. Obviously, the customers of such a professional were all men and they would no doubt take advantage of his skills with the scissors and razor to have their hair cut while having their beards trimmed. Over time, fashions changed and technology made it easier for men to shave themselves, but they still visited the barber on a more or less regular basis to have the hair on their head cut, trimmed or styled. 'Barbers' continued to ply their trade, even though beards were becoming less and less the focus of their professional attention.

From the Middle Ages onwards, barbers offered far more than tonsorial and facial care. If you needed to have a boil lanced, a tooth pulled, an enema or a spot of leeching or bloodletting, the barber was the man you went to see. In fact the dividing line between the barber and professionals we now consider highly qualified medical practitioners was virtually nonexistent. For this reason, barbers were officially referred to as 'barber–surgeons', offering their services  by displaying a 'barber's pole' outside their establishments. This was a pole painted with alternate red and white twisting stripes, which looked very pretty and cheered up an otherwise drab shop exterior. Unfortunately, rather than inviting potential customers to a pleasant experience in personal grooming, it was a grim warning and visual representation of the blood they would lose and the bandages they would probably need if they ventured within.

Batman

With absolutely no relationship to the fictional, comic-book hero of the 1940s, the 'batman' has been an indispensable figure in the British Army since the mid-eighteenth century. His principal duty was to look after the 'bat horse', an alternative name for what we would probably refer to now as a 'pack horse', so-called because it carried 'packs' of kit, stores and equipment. 'Bat horse', on the other hand, reflects how the saddle had been adapted to make carrying the packs easier.

When an officer went to war in the eighteenth and nineteenth centuries he took with him many personal belongings and several changes of clothing and uniform. All this had to be maintained and looked after, frequently under arduous conditions, and of course transported from place to place as the army moved about in both war and peace. The easiest way (and probably the only way) in those days was to have his personal effects strapped to a saddle specially fitted with 'bats', lengths of wood forming a frame around it and to which boxes and cases could be attached. A junior soldier or orderly would have been detailed to take care of the horse, the pack and the saddle as this would then release the officer to get on with the more demanding tasks of military life.

The word 'bat' is derived from the Old French *bast* and the Late Latin *bastum*, both of which originally meant 'a stick' but came to mean a 'pack saddle' as well.

Some etymologists take the derivation as far back as the Ancient Greek *bastazein*, 'to lift', 'to support' – and, considering the context, this association does not sound all that far-fetched.

But there is another surprising suggested etymological relative: the word 'bastard'. The modern form of the word in English is probably an echo of the French *fils de bast*, literally 'son of a packsaddle'. The implication here is that the illegitimate infant was the result of casual congress between some unfortunate maid and a mule driver, who used his packsaddle as a post-coital pillow, then disappeared before dawn.

Beadle

In Anglo-Saxon England the 'beadle' had to be good at what we would now refer to as 'multitasking'. He was a herald or town crier, making proclamations to the populace as and when important news filtered down to the towns and villages from the principal seats of power. It was also his job to deliver important messages to and from personages in authority. And, if all this were not enough, he was a de facto policeman responsible for maintaining order and summoning householders to the local council when required to do so.

The most famous of all beadles has to be Mr Bumble, the parish official (the post was established in the 1590s) who gives Oliver Twist such a hard time in Dickens's novel of the same name. It is an office which has largely died out now, although the occasional anachronistic examples still survive. The universities of Oxford, Cambridge and Durham all employ a beadle (sometimes known by the Latin form of the word, *bedellus*), who carries out various administrative duties and provides information for strangers and visitors to the various colleges. In Canterbury, the King's School still employs a beadle to maintain discipline among the pupils and to reprimand them with a due air of authority if their punctuality for classes or the state of their uniforms leaves something to be desired.

Outside of the world of academe there is also a fascinating hangover from the past to be seen in the Burlington Arcade in London. Here, the beadles are constantly on hand, in their nineteenth-century attire, to ensure that the shoppers in the arcade behave in a seemly and appropriate manner.

The Old English spelling of the word is *bydel*, related to the verb *bēodan*, 'to announce', 'to proclaim', reflecting the Indo-European root *beudh*, 'to be aware', 'to make others aware'. And the association with self-awareness illustrates the connection with one of its cognates, Buddha, a title which literally means 'the enlightened one' or 'the one who is aware'.

> Poetry's unnat'ral; no man ever talked poetry
> 'cept a beadle on boxin' day.
>
> CHARLES DICKENS, *The Pickwick Papers* (1836–37)

Beefeater

We all know the 'beefeaters' of the Tower of London, either because we have visited the famous tower (founded by William the Conqueror in 1066 as a visible sign that England was now his vassal state) or because we have seen pictures of them, resplendent in their Tudor uniforms.

There are several suggestions as to why the Yeoman Warders (as they should be referred to) are known by an epithet suggesting consummate carnivores who probably eat no greens. The one that is usually accepted as the most likely concerns a certain grand duke of Tuscany, Cosimo III de' Medici, who visited the tower in 1669. He is reputed to have been rather over-awed by the splendid physiques of these fine figures of English manhood, and attributed their stature to their being fed on large quantities of beef every day. This would appear to be a reasonable explanation for the derivation of the term, but it does overlook the fact that the word had been in use earlier as a derogatory term for a well-fed servant.

The Yeoman of the Guard was a body set up by Henry VII in 1485 after the Battle of Bosworth to act as a latter-day royal protection team. Within this corps was another distinct unit, the Yeoman Warders, whose task was specifically to look after prisoners in the Tower of London and, at the same time, protect the Crown Jewels. Since Victorian times, however, one of their main roles

has been to act as guides to the thousands of visitors the Tower receives every day.

Since the 1960s one of the Yeoman Warders has enjoyed the magnificent title of Yeoman Warder Raven-master. His job has been to look after the conspiracy of ravens that took up residence in the Tower centuries ago and have never left. And the reason successive monarchs have been so solicitous for the well-being of these birds is because of the legend that has always surrounded them. According to tradition, if the ravens leave the Tower the inner White Tower will come tumbling down and the kingdom will be visited by mayhem and disaster. No doubt the various kings and queens denied that they were in any way superstitious, but thought it wiser to err on the side of caution.

'Take thy beak from out my heart, and take thy form
    from off my door!'
Quoth the Raven 'Nevermore.'

EDGAR ALLAN POE, 'The Raven' (1845)

Best boy

The term was first used in writing, as far as we know,
in 1931, with its specific meaning of an assistant to the
chief electrician in a theatre or on a film set. His duties
include: helping the 'gaffer' or main lighting electrician
with the positioning of the lights, hiring crew, scheduling,
as well as myriad other tasks behind the scenes. He is also
required to stand in for his boss as and when required if
he is involved in other duties or perhaps cannot attend for
one reason or another. All in all, being 'best boy' demands
competence, a thorough understanding of his duties and
a flexible attitude.

The word 'boy' was unknown in English until the
thirteenth century, when it found its way into the language
with the meaning of 'male servant of very low status'. It
was not until the following century that the word was
applied to any young male. Until then the Old English
terms commonly in use were *cnapa* and *cniht*. The former,
cnapa, eventually evolved into 'knave' but it did not
carry the pejorative implications in Saxon times with
which we associate the word today. The latter, *cniht*,

24

progressed up the social scale as the centuries passed by. The lowly servant in Anglo-Saxon England became a youth in military service in the eleventh century; by the sixteenth century he was at the top of the social scale, having been granted permission by the sovereign to use the non-hereditary honorific 'Sir' as a reward for services rendered. This, of course, is the derivation of the word 'knight'.

Many etymologists believe that the word 'boy' is derived from the Old French *embuier*, 'to fetter', derived from the Latin noun *boia*, 'fetter', which can be traced back to the Greek term *boeiai dorai*, meaning 'ox-hide fetters'. This suggests that originally a boy was a servant prevented from running away by being tied up with strips of leather.

> The boy stood on the burning deck
>> Whence all but he had fled;
> The flame that lit the battle's wreck
>> Shone round him o'er the dead.

FELICIA DOROTHEA HEMANS, 'Casabianca' (1826)

Busker

Street performers have provided entertainment to passers-by, in exchange for a small consideration, probably since the dawn of civilization. They demonstrated their skills to bemused onlookers on the streets of Ancient Greece and Rome. Later, in the Middle Ages, all the major towns and cities in France, Germany, Spain and elsewhere played host to itinerant players who would dazzle with their skills in juggling, acrobatics, and magic or virtuosity on any of a variety of musical instruments. In Britain, from about 1860, these latter-day wandering minstrels became known as 'buskers', a title which has survived to the present day.

But the word has changed its meaning. When the verb 'to busk' was first used in the nineteenth century it defined the activities of people who walked around towns offering small items for sale in the pubs and barrooms, rather than providing amusing entertainment. The original use of the word in English, however, was nautical; it had been used previously by sailors to mean 'to cruise about', 'to tack', frequently with the intention of committing acts of piracy.

The word entered English in the mid-seventeenth century from an archaic French word, *busquer*, 'to seek', which has its counterpart in the modern Spanish *buscar*, also meaning 'to seek', 'to keep an eye out for'. Its derivative noun *buscón* can be anything from a 'cheat' to a 'petty thief' and, in its feminine form *buscona,* a 'prostitute'.

A quick look back through the history of busking reveals that quite a few famous people have done a spot of street entertaining before their main career took off. The pop singers Rod Stewart, George Michael and Hayley Westenra all cut their teeth entertaining the crowds with their musical talents before they were 'discovered'. And Piers Brosnan, a future James Bond, performed a fire-eating act on the streets of London before entering drama school.

But the most surprising busker of all has to be Benjamin Franklin (1706–1790), who went on to be an American statesman and inventor of note. He eventually became a highly educated polymath, but as a young man he read out his own poetry and prose to passers-by on the streets of Boston, before his father persuaded him to desist and find more suitable employment.

Butcher

Nowadays, anyone who makes a living out of selling meat, from whatever animal, is referred to as a 'butcher'. But this has not always been the case. In Anglo-Saxon England the term for a seller of animal flesh was 'flesh-monger' (in Old English, *flǣscmangere*), but after the Norman invasion in 1066 the term began to die out and was eventually replaced, by about 1300, with the Anglo-Norman term *boucher*, from the Old French *bochier*. But a *bochier* originally sold nothing but meat from the goat, the Old French for which was *boc*, a word also allied to the modern English 'buck'. The word 'butcher' is thought to have been first used figuratively, in the sense of a brutal killer, in the first half of the sixteenth century.

The butchers' fare, meat, has been synonymous with 'flesh' only since the fourteenth century. Prior to that 'meat' (also spelled *mete*) simply meant 'food' of any kind. Remnants of this usage can be seen in expressions such as 'meat and drink' and 'one man's meat is another man's poison'. Etymologically speaking, there is also a distant connection with the word 'measure', as historically 'meat' was what had been 'meted' or 'measured' out to us as a meal.

> When a butcher tells you his heart bleeds for his country, he has, in fact, no uneasy feeling.
>
> SAMUEL JOHNSON, *Boswell's Life of Johnson* (1791)

Butler

For the vast majority of us, Butler is now a surname (and has been since *c.* 1300), rather than an occupation with which we are likely to be too familiar. But the number of 'Butlers' there are throughout the English-speaking world is an indication of how prevalent the occupation was in times gone by.

As an occupation, the Anglo-French word was *buteillier*, from the Old French *boteillier*, a term applied to servants who served wine to their masters and guests at dinner. Over the years such a person benefited from a series of promotions; at first the *botellier* was upgraded to being in charge of the wine, but eventually he filled the role of head servant in a household. In Victorian and Edwardian Britain, the butler, as it was now spelled, was in a position of considerable authority as he was responsible for the behaviour of all the other servants and for making sure that they performed their allotted tasks satisfactorily.

The original *buteillier* was so called because he was in charge of the *boteilles* or wine vessels, frequently made of leather as opposed to glass. This was a derivation from the Vulgar Latin *butticula*, the diminutive form of the Late Latin *buttis*, meaning a cask or vat (which also gave us the 'butt' of sherry). Eventually, by the mid-fourteenth century, the spelling had changed to the modern 'bottle'. In a high-class restaurant, the person in charge of the wine cellar is frequently referred to as the 'sommelier'. This is another borrowing from French into English, used since 1889 to define the person whose duties include working 'front of house' as a wine waiter, advising customers which wines are most suitable for the dishes they are about to order. But in thirteenth-century France he was a government officer or court official charged with ensuring that adequate provisions were always available to the lords and ladies. And, no doubt, this food and wine would have been transported to their destination on horseback in packs, the French word for which was *somme*, a corruption of the Vulgar Latin *salma* or *sagma*, a packsaddle.

Chancellor of the Exchequer

In most countries of the world the government official responsible for the nation's finances is simply called 'finance minister' or whatever the equivalent is in that country's language. But in Britain we cling to the ancient if somewhat eccentric title of Chancellor of the Exchequer; bearers of this title have looked after the pennies in our pockets since the reign of Henry III (r. 1216–72).

The title Chancellor goes back to Roman times when the *cancellarius* was an officer in the law courts who was responsible for keeping records of all court proceedings. Custom had it that he remained seated behind the *cancelli* or lattice-work screen, out of sight of the judge, from which the title of his office was derived.

Another word derived from *cancelli* was the verb *cancellare*, 'to make a lattice-work structure'. And, as such structures were mainly used for the purpose of fencing off areas of a building or piece of land, the verb soon acquired an additional meaning: to enclose. This is further related to another noun, *carcer*, 'prison', the root of our word 'incarceration'. Sometimes, of course, a *cancellarius* would, during the course of his record-keeping, have to correct certain words or sentences. He would frequently do this by making a criss-cross or lattice pattern over the offending part of the document, hence the origin of our verb 'to cancel'.

The word 'exchequer' is no less interesting from an etymological point of view. We borrowed the term from the Old French *eschequier*, which primarily meant 'a chess board'. The connection here is that in the Middle Ages accounts were calculated by moving counters around this chequered board or *eschequier*, which was also the term for the board on which *échecs*, the game we know as chess, was played.

Chandler

This is not a word we hear much in the modern world, though as recently as the 1950s and 1960s almost every high street in every town in the country would have had a chandler's shop. The goods these shops sold (buckets, tin baths, cleaning fluids, soaps, brushes of all kinds, watering cans, etc.) are now usually found down one of the aisles in a DIY superstore, so the word itself has fallen into disuse.

In the Middle Ages, however, it was a very different story. The fourteenth-century chandler (the word was borrowed from the Old French *chandelier*) was the man who made or sold candles which would help the local community see what they were doing or where they were going on dark nights. Or, alternatively, he could have been employed in a large house, owned by a local landowner or member of the nobility, to be in charge of the lighting arrangements throughout the day and night.

By the 1590s the chandlers had broadened their horizons a little and had begun selling provisions of various sorts to such an extent that there was little difference between them and other merchants. In the age of sail they provided candles for ships, but also much of the other equipment the sailors would need while at sea. Even today the 'ship's chandler' still exists, but now provides food, stores, ropes and all the paraphernalia required to keep the vessel clean, tidy and generally 'shipshape and Bristol fashion'.

The Old French word *chandelier* came from the word *chandelle* and the Latin for 'candle', *candela*. And this noun was derived from the verb *candere*, meaning 'to be bright', 'to shine'. However, tracing the words back to their supposed Indo-European root we find **kand*, which produced other words cognate with 'candle' that might not appear immediately to be connected in any way. One such is 'candid', now meaning 'open', 'truthful', but originally it simply meant 'bright' or even 'white'. And a man in Ancient Rome who walked around in a *candida toga* (a white toga), trying to drum up support or secure people's votes, gave us the modern word 'candidate'.

A 'chandelier', as used in modern English meaning a many-branched support for candles or a collection of light bulbs, has been a feature of the language only since the eighteenth century.

> How far that little candle throws its beams!
> So shines a good deed in a naughty world.
>> WILLIAM SHAKESPEARE, *The Merchant of Venice*
>> (1596–99), 5.1

Chaperon(e)

This is a perfect example of how a misspelling can become the accepted form. When the word entered English in the fourteenth century it was spelled 'chaperon' (the *OED* still offers it as an alternative) and simply meant 'hood'. By the eighteenth century it was being used with the additional figurative meaning of 'protector', particularly of young ladies whose virtue was deemed to be at risk if they left the house unaccompanied. As these 'protectors' were almost always, if not exclusively, women of a certain age, it was thought that the word should look more 'feminine' and so a final 'e' was added and this has become the more normal form of the word.

'Chaperon' was a direct borrowing from the French, for whom it was the diminutive form of *chape*, a cap or hood (hence also the modern French *chapeau*). This in turn was borrowed from the Late Latin *cappa*, also a protective covering for the head, although in English *chape* acquired the additional meaning of 'a metal protective plate', particularly the metal covering at the end of a scabbard.

But there is a much more romantic possibility. It has been suggested that a 'chaperon(e)' takes her title from falconry. The little hood fitted over a falcon's head was also known as a 'chaperon' and its purpose was to stop the bird flying away and seeking its freedom. The same reasoning was behind the employment of a matron for a young damsel who was perhaps 'straining at the jesses' and wished to 'spread her wings'.

Chapman

Not so very long ago 'chap' was an informal term for a man, and phrases such as 'he's a decent sort of chap' and 'he's a friendly chap' would have been quite common. In the plural it was often used to address a group of men, as in 'Hello, chaps.' Nowadays this all sounds quite dated and the American custom of referring to just about everybody as 'guy' or 'guys' seems to have swamped the older term, which had excellent Anglo-Saxon credentials.

'Chap' was a shortened form of 'chapman', which survives today mainly as a surname, but in Anglo-Saxon England a *cēapman* was an itinerant peddler. By the thirteenth century, however, it had undergone a complete reversal in meaning; it now referred not to the trader but to the customer. And, of course, when the customer entered the shop he would be looking for a 'good deal', which in medieval England was known as a *good cheape*, based on the Old English *cēap*, 'bargain, price, market'. And this explains why, in modern English, if we manage to buy something for far less than we expected to pay, we describe it as being 'cheap'. This use of the word has been with us since the fifteenth century.

But the word has also survived in other contexts. The association of the Old English *cēap* with anything to do with buying and selling meant that it was synonymous with a 'market'. We see this clearly in many place names, such as Chepstow (originally Cheap stow, 'market place') and, in its slightly corrupted form, 'chipping', as in Chipping Norton, Chipping Sodbury, and so on.

In modern English, if we cannot make our minds up about something, we are often accused of 'chopping and changing'. Even this non-commercial sounding expression has its roots in the world of trade: 'chop' here is a variant of the Old English *cēapian*, 'to sell'; the original phrase was 'chap and change', which simply meant 'to sell and exchange' or 'to barter'.

> Oh! God! That bread should be so dear,
> And flesh and blood so cheap!
>
> THOMAS HOOD, 'The Song of the Shirt' (1843)

Charwoman

In the sixteenth century it became the custom to refer to women who were employed on an irregular basis to perform odd jobs or 'chores' (a corruption of 'char') around the house as 'charwomen', 'charladies' or simply 'chars' (the first recorded use of the word was in 1379). The term was quite common in the UK until the 1950s when it was gradually replaced by alternative terms such as 'ladies who do', 'daily woman' or simply 'daily'.

Unlike maids or housekeepers, who tended to live on the premises, charwomen came and went, as and when they were required to do a spot of cleaning, dusting or tidying up, thus freeing the other staff from the more menial jobs and allowing them to get on with their main tasks to ensure the smooth running of the household. In offices, hospitals and factories, charwomen or charladies still perform their important roles, but are more usually referred to now as 'cleaners'.

The basis of the word is 'char', which in Middle English meant a 'turn of work', 'a task demanding just a brief period of time'. This was derived from the Old English *cer* or *cierr*, meaning 'time' or 'occasion', and the associated verb *cierran*, 'to turn'. We might even say that 'charwoman' combines both meanings: she would appear for a short 'time' and do her 'turn' of work.

But there is also a rather unsuspected link here to another expression. In the Middle Ages, if one left the door to a house or room *on char* it meant that the door was slightly open and free to swing or 'turn' on the hinges. By 1718 this term had evolved into 'on a jar' or 'on the jar', providing us with the modern expression 'ajar'.

Chauffeur

Chauffeurs nowadays tend to be uniformed, professional drivers who drive important and/or rich people from where they are to where they want to be. But when the term was first used at the very end of the nineteenth century, it was a nickname. As the first motorcars were steam-driven the drivers were mockingly referred to in France as *chauffeurs*, after the stokers on boats and ships who spent their days shovelling coal into the furnaces that produced the steam that moved the pistons that turned the wheels.

When the first petrol engines were developed at the beginning of the twentieth century, a chauffeur's responsibilities changed considerably. He no longer had to stoke a fire to produce steam but, before the days of electric ignition, he had to start the engines by a laborious process of heating specially designed tubes and inserting them into the engine to produce the spark that set things off. Once this had been achieved, the tubes were kept at a constant temperature by the engine's own compression cycle and the chauffeur could assume his other main duty – steering the car.

The word 'chauffeur' was originally French. It was derived from the Old French verb *chaufer*, 'to heat', which in turn came from the Vulgar Latin *calefare* and the Latin *calefacere*, both of which meant 'to heat'. The same Latin words gave us 'calorie', 'cauldron' and even 'chowder', a thick fish soup cooked in a hot pot or cauldron. Less obviously, the verb 'to chafe' (to heat up by rubbing) is also a relative, as is the adjective 'nonchalant', absorbed into English from French in 1734 to describe a person's cool, as opposed to heated, response to a given situation.

Chef

The French expression *chef de cuisine* (head of the kitchen) was adopted into English in the nineteenth century and has been used ever since to denote the person responsible for the smooth running of any restaurant and the quality of the food they serve to their customers.

The word 'chef' is a direct linguistic descendant of the Vulgar Latin *capum* and the Latin *caput*, meaning 'head'. It is also closely connected to 'chief' (which entered English in the early fourteenth century) and the Late Latin *capitaneus*, from which English derived the noun 'captain', also in the fourteenth century. If we take things a little further, we see that 'chef' is also directly related to the Italian *cappuccino*, the frothy coffee so-called either because it has a 'head' on it or because its colour resembles that of a Capuchin friar's head covering. And there are those in the etymology community who maintain that another cognate is the word 'cabbage', which, they argue, takes its name from the fact that its shape resembles that of a human head.

'Cook' is also an English word that can trace its origins back to Latin. The man who prepared the food in Ancient Rome was known as a *coquus*, who took his occupational title from the verb *coquere*, 'to cook' or 'to prepare' food. And the person for whom a *coquus* cooked would, after a no doubt splendid meal, take time to digest what he had just enjoyed. The Latin verb for this intestinal process was *concoquere*, which, in the sixteenth century, gave English the noun 'concoction'.

> 'tis an ill cook that cannot lick his own fingers.
> WILLIAM SHAKESPEARE, *Romeo and Juliet* (1595?), 4.2

Chimney sweep

The first recorded mention of chimney sweeps is in 1796 (as early as 1610 they were called 'chimney sweepers'), a time when people were being swallowed up by the Industrial Revolution and the resulting increased urbanization. Houses were built close together and the main source of heating was coal, which produced vast amounts of soot in combination with creosote, a highly flammable by-product of burning fossil fuels. So, it was the chimney sweeps' vitally important job to keep the soot to a minimum; but there was a problem. Because many of the chimneys were too narrow for adults to squeeze into, orphan boys were taken on as 'apprentices' (some as young as four years old) and made to climb up inside the chimneys, sweeping away the soot as they got higher and higher. It was an extremely cruel form of employment as the children were exposed to all sorts of perils. There was the ever-present danger of falling; the possibility of suffocation; the threat of being trapped; and, if this were not enough, soot is carcinogenic and many succumbed to what came to be known as 'chimney sweeps' carcinoma'. It was not until 1875 that it became illegal to employ children as chimney sweeps.

'Chimney' was a late-thirteenth-century borrowing of the Old French *cheminee*, which had several meanings. It could refer to the fireplace, the room in which the fire was situated, or, from the twelfth century onwards, the chimney stack. The Old French word was in turn borrowed from the Late Latin *caminata*, 'fire place', a derivative of the Greek *kaminos*, 'furnace', 'stove' or 'flue'. It is the last of these which is the probable link between a stove in Ancient Athens and a modern chimney.

Another link is with the word 'chamber', derived from the Late Latin *camera caminata*, 'heated room', but literally 'the room where the fireplace is'.

Golden lads and girls all must,
As chimney-sweepers, come to dust.

WILLIAM SHAKESPEARE, *Cymbeline* (1611), 4.2

Cloud architect

This is just one of the very many expressions that the world of computing has given us over the past few decades. It is a metaphorical reference to the way in which remote servers cooperate with each other over the Internet. For non-specialists, the best way to think of it is as a central-ized digital storage system for the vast amount of data we load onto our computers every day.

But, of course, such a complicated system requires a high degree of planning, maintenance and management, and it is the job of a company's 'cloud architect' to super-vise the component tasks to ensure the smooth running of the service. The first reference to such an employee was in 1996, but the term did not become widely used until after the year 2000.

The word 'cloud' itself has gone through quite a lot of change since it was first used centuries ago by the Anglo-Saxons. For them, a *clūd* was not the billowy, fluffy thing in the sky; it had a far more terrestrial meaning – a lump of rock or pile of earth. Our ancestors were obviously struck by how a rock could resemble a cloud in shape, so that eventually the heavenly connection prevailed and the earth-bound association was forgotten.

It was only in the thirteenth century that the word acquired the meaning we attach to it today; our 'cloud' was referred to in Old English as *weolcn*, surviving in archaic or poetic language as 'welkin'.

For the term 'architect' we have to thank the Ancient Greeks. They took two words, *archein*, 'to rule', 'to be in charge of', and *tektōn*, 'builder', and combined them to form *architektōn*, literally meaning 'builder in charge'. Originally, these highly skilled craftsmen would have overseen the construction of magnificent buildings such as the Acropolis in Ancient Athens. Little did they know that their job titles would have such significance for the technology of the twenty-first century.

Coach

Few people reading or hearing that 'the team coach travelled to the ground with the players on the team coach' would fail to understand the meaning; the person responsible for making sure that the team was match-fit travelled to the venue together with the players on the same means of transport. How, then, did 'coach' come to have two such diverse meanings?

The answer lies in a small village in Hungary where, in the fifteenth century, a peasant craftsman had a brilliant idea. The village in question was Kocs (pronounced 'kotch') and the craftsman earned his living by making carts and carriages. One day it occurred to him to attach the body of a carriage to the wheel axles by a system of springs; the result was as he expected. The new carriage gave travellers a far smoother ride and made journeys over the unmetalled roads less arduous and far more comfortable.

The Hungarian for such a mode of transport was *kocsi széker*, 'carriage from Kocs', but as the new means of transport became famous throughout Europe, and eventually the world, the name was shortened to (with varying spellings) 'coach'.

In 1830 at the University of Oxford, the word acquired a more figurative meaning when the term 'coach' was applied to tutors, who were responsible for 'driving' students along the metaphorical road that led to examination success. By 1860 this usage had spread to the world of sport, which brings us back to an additional, modern application of the word.

Colporteur

The period of history generally referred to as the Reformation was one of tremendous ideological and social upheaval. The old beliefs were brought into question and factionalism ushered in a degree of social upheaval that left its mark, still evident today, on the whole of Europe. And the new religious groups that emerged over the next few centuries all wanted to preach their own brand of whatever belief they espoused.

From the early 1700s one of the methods chosen for spreading religious propaganda was termed 'colporterage'.

This was a distribution system involving 'colporteurs' or 'colporters' who roamed the length and breadth of the country selling religious tracts and modestly priced Bibles from bags suspended around their necks. Eventually, the more enterprising added cheap versions of popular, non-religious publications of the day to the books they had on offer. No doubt this proved a popular move among people who lived in more remote communities and for whom a visit to a bookshop involved a time-consuming, and possibly expensive, trip to the nearest town or city.

The derivation of this word is contentious. Some etymologists are convinced that the word comprises two parts: 'col' from the French and Latin for neck (*col* and *collum* respectively) and the Latin verb *portare*, 'to carry'. Others, however, are of the opinion that it is a distorted version of the derivative Latin verb *comportare*, 'to carry', 'to collect', 'to bring together', implying that a 'colporteur' was simply a hawker who carried all his merchandise with him.

There is absolutely no connection with the American songwriter Cole Porter (1891–1964). It was by pure coincidence that his parents named him Cole Albert Porter; the connection with itinerant booksellers is merely auditory.

A good book is the precious life-blood of a master-spirit, embalmed and treasured up on purpose to a life beyond life.

JOHN MILTON, *Areopagitica* (1644)

Conductor

Until relatively recently there were two types of conductor. There was the man (or, less commonly, woman) who waved a baton in front of an orchestra, making sure that each individual musician kept time so that the whole ensemble produced harmonious music. This use of the word has existed in English since 1784.

Until the 1970s or early 1980s there was also the man (the women in this role were often referred to as 'clippies') who collected the fares from, and issued tickets to, the passengers on a bus. Nowadays, buses tend to be manned by one person who doubles up as both the driver and the collector of fares.

When the word was adopted into English in the 1520s it simply meant a 'military leader'. It was a borrowing of the Middle French term *conductour*, itself taken from the Latin verb *conducere*, 'to bring together', 'to gather', implying that a leader (particularly in a military context) was the strongman at the front who brought his army together before leading it into battle. Perhaps a little oddly, however, the Latin noun *conductor* did not have any military connotations. It was more of a commercial term meaning 'contractor' or 'one who hires'.

The Latin noun was formed from the verb *conducere*, comprising the prefix *con*, 'with', 'together', and the basic verb *ducere*, 'to lead', 'to draw' (also seen in words such as 'viaduct', 'aqueduct', 'reduction'). It would appear, therefore, that the original 'conductors' in Ancient Rome 'drew people' together for reasons of trade or business.

But there was also another Latin noun derived from the same verb: *dux* (genitive *ducis*), who would also have been the leader of a land army or a naval commander. Eventually this word filtered into English too, but is more recognizable today as 'duke'. In the twelfth century it would have applied to a sovereign prince or the ruler of a 'duchy', and by the fourteenth it had become a hereditary title among the nobility.

> 'And everybody praised the Duke,
> Who this great fight did win.'
> 'But what good came of it at last?'
> Quoth little Peterkin.
>
> ROBERT SOUTHEY, 'The Battle of Blenheim' (1798)

Constable

The idea of a constable being a representative of the law is a relatively modern one. The first time the title was used with the meaning we attach to it today – that is, a police officer – was in 1836, although it was applied as early as *c.* 1600 to men chosen for minor duties connected with upholding the law of the land.

If we go back to the Middle Ages we find that *c.* 1200 a constable was a chief household officer, which frequently included being the governor of a royal castle. From 1300 it was a term applied to office-holders we would now think of more as 'justices of the peace'. The word came into English in the Middle Ages from Old French, which had *conestable*, borrowed from Medieval Latin *conestabulus*, in turn derived from the Late Latin *comes stabuli*.

Comes stabuli was a phrase combining *comes*, 'companion', 'attendant' or even 'fellow traveller', and *stabuli*, the Late Latin for 'of the stable'. In other words, the original 'constables' in England were men tasked with the supervision and care of the stables and horses therein.

The colloquial epithet for a constable, a 'copper', was first recorded as being used among the criminal fraternity in London in 1846 and is derived from the Latin *capere*, 'to take' or 'to seize'.

> When constabulary duty's to be done …
> A policeman's lot is not a happy one.
>   W.S. GILBERT, *The Pirates of Penzance* (1879)

Controller

The noun 'controller' has been used in a technical context with the meaning of 'that which restrains or governs' only since 1867, although the verb from which it is derived has been used in English since the fifteenth century. Both the verb and the noun have been through a rather tortuous history and development.

In Middle English a controller was strictly defined as a person who kept a duplicate register of accounts and was usually to be found in the king's household keeping a close eye on the ruler's income and expenditure. This description, however, is a further development in the evolution of the word; in Anglo-Norman the word used was *contrerollour*, derived from the verb *contreroller*, which had the specific meaning of 'to check accounts by comparing the register with a duplicate register'. And Medieval Latin, the origin of both these words, had the verb *contrarotulare*, 'to keep a copy of a roll', from the noun *contrarotulus*, 'a copy of a roll'. This noun comprised *contra*, 'against', and *rotulus*, 'a roll', which itself was directly derived from the Latin *rota*, 'a wheel'.

The association with a wheel is self-evident; at the time when the word entered English it was the custom for all accounts to be prepared and maintained in scroll form, which, when not being examined, could be 'rolled up' and stored in a suitable place for safekeeping.

Cooper

Cooperage is very much a dying art in Britain now and most people probably know the term 'cooper' only as a surname. But in the fourteenth century 'cooper' became the generally accepted term in English for the man who made and repaired barrels and 'coops', as baskets were frequently referred to in those days.

Historically, coopers divided themselves into three groups: 'dry', 'wet' and 'white'. The first group made barrels or casks specifically for the storage or transport of dry food such as grain or wheat. The second made the barrels that served as receptacles for ale, wines and so on. The 'white' coopers traditionally confined their activities to producing the pails and buckets used on farms during milking or for carrying water from the well.

The word is a borrowing of the Dutch *kuip*, 'vat' or 'tub', itself a derivation of the Medieval Latin *cōpa*, 'a tun', 'a barrel', which is a variant of the Latin *cūpa*, 'cask' or 'butt'. Tracing the history of the word a little further back we find that *cūpa* is directly related to the Greek *cupellon*, meaning a  goblet or large drinking vessel. And both examples from classical antiquity are, theoretically at least, linked to the Indo-European root **keup*, 'hollow' or 'curved', and directly related to our words 'cup', 'cowl' and even 'cow'.

In the fifteenth century the word 'coop' was also being used to describe the cage in which poultry was kept, and by the sixteenth it was applied generally to any place of confinement. This is why we can talk even now of 'being cooped up' when we mean we feel trapped inside a building and feel the desperate need to escape.

The prevalence of surnames found in other European
languages associated with barrel-making suggest that
the skills the cooper had to offer were in great demand.
Consider the following:

French	Tonnellier
German	Binder/Fassbender
Dutch	Kuiper
Hungarian	Kádár
Spanish	Cubero
Russian	Bondarev
Ukrainian	Bondarenko
Danish	Bødker
Greek	Varelas

||||||||||||||||||||||||||||||||||||||||||||||||||||||||||||||||||||||||||||||||||||||||||||||||||||||||||

Cordwainer

In Anglo-Saxon England the man who made shoes for his
clients was known as a *scōhere* (shoe-er) or *scōwyrhta* (shoe
wright), but when the Crusades began in 1096 the days
of the traditional shoemaker were numbered. Soldiers,
crossing and recrossing Europe on their way to and from
the holy sites they were supposed to be defending, came
into contact with other cultures and brought back what
we would think of today as souvenirs.

One of these mementoes was a kind of leather which
was far superior to anything the traditional shoemakers
of England had seen previously. This was a material
produced in Córdoba, the capital of Moorish Spain. It
became so popular with leather workers back home in

England that 'cordouan' (a corruption of the Spanish adjective *cordobano*) leather was soon regarded as the best that money could buy; shoes made from it became the 'must have' articles for those who could afford them. By 1100 the makers of this wonderful footwear were being referred to as 'cordwainers'; they became so numerous and respected in society that the first English Guild of Cordwainers was founded in Oxford in 1131. A century and a half later, in 1272, the Worshipful Company of Cordwainers received its ordinances; it has survived to the present day.

But the cordwainers have another claim to fame. Before 1300 the tradition had been not to distinguish between shoes intended for the right foot and those to be worn on the left; shoes were simply designed to be worn on either foot. But at the beginning of the fourteenth century, cordwainers had the idea of fashioning shoes as we know them today – with a right and left bias.

The term 'cobbler' (of unknown origin) did not appear before the thirteenth century and referred only to tradesmen who repaired shoes, not to those who made them.

Coroner

Nowadays the principal duties of the coroner are twofold: he or she is responsible for establishing exactly how the deceased died in cases where the death is unexpected, violent or suspicious; as part of this process the coroner is also required to determine the identity of the deceased beyond all doubt.

A third duty of a coroner is to safeguard the property of the Crown (such as in cases of treasure trove), a responsibility that links him or her directly with the origins of the profession, dating back to the Middle Ages. In those days a coroner was less interested in how a victim of sudden death met their end than what subsequently happened to their property. His job was to make sure that any money or property owing to the monarch was not appropriated by the lord of the manor or anybody else who might have got his hands on it. It was not until the seventeenth century that his chief role was to establish cause of death and determine whether or not criminality should be suspected.

The original function of a coroner as a protector of Crown property is a clue to the etymology of the title. The office of coroner was established in England in 1194 and the man appointed to the post was officially known by his Latin title *custos placitorum coronae* (the guardian of the pleas of the Crown). This had been shortened to *coronarius* by the thirteenth century and was abbreviated again, in the fifteenth, to 'crowner'.

The Latin noun at play here, *corona* (from the Greek *korōnē*, 'anything curved or bent'), is a perfect example of how a simple word can acquire greater hierarchical status as it moves up the social scale. A *corona* in Ancient Rome began life as a simple garland, perhaps worn on the head (remember the 'crown of thorns'?) and then, over time, came to mean a chaplet, or little hat.

It was not until the twelfth century that the word 'crown' was used figuratively in England to mean 'royal authority'.

> Uneasy lies the head that wears a crown.
> WILLIAM SHAKESPEARE, *2 Henry IV* (1597?), 3.1

Costermonger

When the word 'costermonger' entered English in the very early sixteenth century, it was applied specifically to itinerant traders who hawked their wares around the streets of London in baskets or on handcarts. Originally, these traders sold only apples, but fairly soon the word was being used with the more general meaning of a seller of all fruits and vegetables. Over the years the meaning expanded even further until it included anyone who sold apples, pears, carrots and so on from a barrow or stall on a marketplace, and this sense has been retained up to the present day.

From an etymological point of view, the word 'coster-monger' consists of two distinct parts. The second element, 'monger', is used only as a suffix and appears in modern English words such as 'fishmonger', 'ironmonger', 'cheese-monger'. It also features in such expressions, usually with a pejorative or at least uncomplimentary tinge, as 'warmonger' or 'scandalmonger'.

'Monger' entered English from a Germanic root (Old English had *mangian*, 'to traffic', and *mangere* for a 'trader') related directly to the Latin *mango*, 'a dealer', a term that was frequently applied to anyone who profited from the slave trade. And the Latin noun is closely allied to the Greek verb *magganein* (pronounced 'manganein'), 'to trick', 'to deceive by sleight of hand'. Is this perhaps a reflection of the poor esteem in which market traders were held in days gone by?

The first part of the word, 'coster', was originally 'costard' when it found its way into English in the four-teenth century and defined a variety of large apple. It took its name not from its size but from the prominent protuberances running down its sides, making the apple look as if it had 'ribs'. And this is the derivation of 'costard', from the Anglo-Norman *coste* and the Latin *costa*, both of which meant 'rib'.

> [V]irtue is of so little regard in these costermongers' times that true valour is turned bearherd.
>
> WILLIAM SHAKESPEARE, *2 Henry IV* (1597?), 1.2

Croupier

Habitués of casinos will be well acquainted with this word. The croupier, of course, is the lady or gentleman who stands at the gaming table and gathers in the chips or deals the cards as the punters place their bets. But this has been the case only since 1731. Prior to that the 'croupier' played the role of a gambler's assistant, standing behind the gambler, offering advice and money as and when one or other commodity was required. And the name was taken from the role played by the original croupiers – that is, horseback pillion riders who sat on the horse's rump, the French term for which is *la croupe*. The original position occupied by the croupier in a gambling establishment is also the reason we speak, even today, of 'backing' someone financially.

> Cupid and my Campaspe played
> At cards for kisses; Cupid paid.
>
> JOHN LYLY, *Campaspe* (1584), 3.5

Currier

In fourteenth-century England a 'currier' was a man whose job it was to take a piece of tanned leather and dress it – that is, make it pliable, waterproof and ready for use. It was then passed on to shoemakers, cobblers, clothiers, saddle-makers or whoever else needed it for whatever product they intended to make with it.

The original spelling of the word in English was *curayour*, a variation of the Old French *corier*, a word which worked its way down from the Latin, *coriarius*, meaning 'pertaining to leather' or 'a tanner'. This in turn was derived from the noun *corium*, the normal Latin word for 'hide' or 'leather', from the Indo-European root *sker*, 'to cut'; a reminder that skin or hide has to be 'cut' off a dead animal.

And the Latin term for a man who earned a living cutting hides off animals has several cognates still evident in English and other languages today. Presumably, his knife would have to be 'sharp', he might have been wearing a 'shirt' as he flayed a dead cow, and his wife might have worn a 'skirt' as she looked after the home; all words derived from the Indo-European *sker*. A knife has to be 'sharp' if it is to cut, and a 'shirt' and a 'skirt' (originally the same word) are articles of clothing which have been 'cut' from a length of cloth.

The derivative surname, Curry, first appeared in English in the thirteenth century.

> I am indeed, sir, a surgeon to old shoes: when they are in great danger I recover them. As proper men as ever trod upon neat's leather* have gone upon my handiwork.
>
> WILLIAM SHAKESPEARE, *Julius Caesar* (1599), I.I

---

* 'Neat' is an archaic term for cattle.

Dentist

Very few of us look forward to visiting the dentist, even though we recognize that regular check-ups are for our own good. The better the state of our teeth, the more easily we can enjoy eating, even if we are totally unaware that 'teeth' and 'eat' are words very closely connected by etymology.

The dentist, as opposed to the barber–surgeon, was first recognized as a professional in his own right in Europe as the Middle Ages began to recede into the past, but it was not until the eighteenth century that the term was used. In France, in 1728, Pierre Fauchard (now regarded as the father of modern dentistry) published the first textbook on the subject which could be deemed 'scientific' in its approach, *Le Chirugien Dentiste*, 'The Surgeon Dentist'.

'Dentist' is derived from the Latin for 'tooth', *dens* (genitive *dentis*), a relative of the Greek *odous* (genitive *odontos*), and the English, Latin and Greek words are all related to the Indo-European *ed, 'to eat'. In other words, the basic historical idea behind the act of eating is simply 'using one's teeth'.

By comparison, other languages such as French and Italian have *manger* and *mangiare* respectively for 'to eat', words which are directly related to 'mandible', suggesting that the French and Italians prefer to think of eating as 'using one's jaws'.

Closely connected with the noun *dens* was the Latin verb *edere*, which gave English the words 'to eat' and 'edible'. But the Romans also had an alternative (etymologically related) form of this verb: *esse*, which has an interesting derivative in English. The past participle of the verb, *esus*, combined with the prefix *ob*, meaning 'because of', 'on account of', to produce the Latin adjective *obesus*, which is our word 'obese'.

> Who trusted God was love indeed
>   And love Creation's final law –
>   Tho' Nature, red in tooth and claw
> With ravine, shriek'd against his creed
>
> ALFRED, LORD TENNYSON, *In Memoriam* (1850)

Detective

In the middle of the nineteenth century a new expression came into use among those responsible for maintaining law and order in England: 'detective policeman'. Within a short period of time 'policeman' was dropped and the adjective became the noun as we use it today. And this new breed of policeman was distinguished from his colleagues by the fact that he did not wear a uniform and concentrated on discovering who had committed a particular crime or crimes, frequently working 'under cover' in order to do so. Traffic duties and pounding the beat were duties left to the uniformed branch. The operative word here is 'discover', as it is directly linked in meaning to the Latin origin of the word 'detective'. In Latin, the verb *tegere* meant 'to cover' and its opposite, *detegere*, meant 'to remove the cover from', or, in other words, 'to uncover', which is simply an alternative form of 'discover'. One of the Latin nouns associated here is *tegmen*, 'cover', which is cognate with nouns in many European languages, all associated with 'covering'. Ancient Greek had *stegos*, 'roof' (allied to 'stegosauros', a 'covered' lizard), German has *Dach* for 'roof', and English has 'thatch' for a particular type of roof made of reeds. A little further afield, other cognates are the Irish Gaelic *teach* and the Welsh *ty*, both of which simply mean 'house'.

Detectives spend their days (and frequently nights) conducting 'investigations', although these days perhaps not quite so literally as might once have been the case. 'Investigation' is derived from the Latin *vestigium*, 'footprint', 'trace' (the same word gave us 'vestige'); thus the original 'investigators' were probably our ancestors spending much of their time following the footprints of animals to 'detect' which way they were heading and 'discover' where they were hiding. Good 'detective work' and a successfully concluded 'investigation' in those days meant meat on the table (or perhaps just the floor of the cave) for the whole family.

A synonymous, colloquial word for a detective is 'sleuth', which first appeared in English in the nineteenth century, and was originally the Old Norse *slóth*, also meaning a 'trail'.

Doctor

To most people the doctor is the person they turn to when they have a medical problem and need advice on how to deal with it. But this has not always been the case. When the word was first used in English in about the year 1300 the title was reserved for elders of the church; it had been borrowed from the Old French *doctor*, from the medieval Latin *doctor*, meaning 'religious teacher' or 'scholar'. The derivative verb at play here is the Latin *docere*, 'to teach', which, incidentally, is directly related to the adjective 'docile', originally meaning 'capable of being taught'.

The association with academe and the world of learning survives today in the universities, where the highest degrees are referred to as 'doctorates' and those who are awarded one are entitled to be addressed as 'doctor'.

The word 'doctor' has been linked to the medical profession only since the early fifteenth century; even then it was not commonly used to designate a physician until the late sixteenth. Prior to that, a common term was still the Old English *lǽce*, or 'leech', which is thought by some etymologists to be the same word as the blood-sucking worm, the leech, highly regarded for its supposed medical efficacy until relatively recently. In fact, whether the link between the physician and the worm is etymologically reliable or not, there is no getting away from the fact that the practical connection was real. The Old English term for the art of healing was *lǣcecræft*; 'a physician's skill' could also be translated as 'skill with leeches'.

And there is another clue. The fourth finger of either hand was referred to in Old English as the *lǣcefinger* or 'leech finger', so-called because it was believed that a vein ran from it all the way to the heart. This would no doubt have been vitally important for a 'leech' looking for somewhere to apply the 'leech'.

> God heals, and the physician hath the thanks.
> GEORGE HERBERT, *Jacula Prudentum* (1640)

Drug czar

The word 'czar' is Slavonic in origin, but is used with increasing regularity in the USA and Britain as a title for anyone appointed to a position of authority. In 1882 it was first applied outside Europe to the president of the USA, Andrew Johnson (1808–1875), possibly because of his vehement antipathy towards those who fought to abolish slavery. It is still used widely in America in a variety of social contexts, so that unofficial titles such as 'pot czar', 'marijuana czar', can be found, as well as the more recent versions such as 'cybersecurity czar' and 'terrorism czar'. In the UK we now have the terms 'drug czar', 'families czar' and 'homelessness czar'.

But there is a problem: the spelling 'czar' is incorrect. A certain sixteenth-century Austrian diplomat, Baron von Herberstein (1486–1566), published a book about Muscovy (as Russia was then known) entitled *Rerum Muscovitarum commentarii* (*Comments on Muscovite Matters*). This appeared in English translation in 1555, containing the word 'czar', and the spelling has persisted ever since. It would appear that the baron's knowledge of Muscovite affairs was reasonably sound, but his understanding of the language was rather limited.

The spelling 'czar' does not reflect the sound of the Russian word *tsar*; 'tsar' (now the preferred spelling) does. It is a derivative, via German, of the Latin term applied to several of the Roman emperors, *Caesar*. The first person to borrow the term in Muscovy was Ivan IV ('the Terrible'), who was crowned 'Tsar of all the Russias' in 1547; prior to this rulers in Russia were titled Grand Prince or Grand Duke.

There is also a common misconception regarding the wives of the tsars. They are frequently referred to as the 'czarina', but there are two mistakes here. The first is the same misspelling as with 'czar'; the second is with the word itself. In Russian in the days leading up to the 1917 Revolution the wife of the tsar was known as the *tsaritsa*; *tsarina* did not exist. It found favour outside Russia largely due to the Germans and Italians, who referred to the lady as *Zarin* and *Czarina* respectively.

Editor

In the newspaper world an editor can be the person running a small-scale operation such as a local newspaper or whoever is in charge of a vast organization gathering news from all over the world and distributing it in print form on a daily or weekly basis. Such people can wield considerable power and, by adding clearly defined political and social opinions to the dissemination of news, influence the way in which their readers think and vote.

But the word has not always had this meaning. In the seventeenth century, when the word entered English, it was applied to people we now refer to as 'publishers'. In the eighteenth century an 'editor' was the person who prepared an author's handwritten document for publication, no doubt checking for spelling and grammar errors and perhaps suggesting ways of improving the original style. It was not until 1803 that the term 'editor' became associated mainly with newspaper bosses.

For the derivation of the word we have to turn to Latin, as it is directly linked to the Latin verb *edere*, a contraction of *ex*, 'out', and *dere*, a form of the verb *dare*, 'to give'. And the derivative noun *editor*, for the Romans, was literally someone who 'gave out' information, or made it public, much as it is to us today.

But the Romans also used another verb with a similar meaning, *publicare*, 'to make public' or, literally, 'to make available to the *populus* or people'. *Publicare* eventually made its way to other parts of Europe and reappeared in Old French as *puplier*, then into Middle English as *puplise*, and finally into modern English as 'publish'. But, confusingly, the modern French for 'publisher' is *éditeur*.

> This is the editorial age, and the most intellectual of all ages
>
> JAMES GORDON BENNETT SR (1795–1872)

Electrician

Electricians play a crucial part in societies throughout the world. Their understanding of how electricity works means that the generators function as they should, that power is available to the whole of industry, and that when we flick a switch the light comes on or the kettle boils. Before the advent of electricians, life was very different and almost impossible for us to imagine now.

In 1751, when the term 'electricians' was first used it referred to a small group of scientists who were devoting their time to studying this strange natural power which had been identified but was little understood. It was not until 1869 that this source of energy had been harnessed sufficiently for it to be put to good use by 'electricians', as we understand the word today.

But, perhaps surprisingly, 'electricity' was known to exist, even though it had not been named as such, in ancient times. The Ancient Egyptians knew that there was one particular fish (they called it 'the Thunderer'), swimming about in the Nile that could give anyone who touched it a nasty shock. The Ancient Greeks, Romans and Arabs all knew 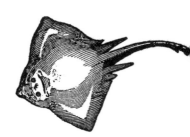 that certain fish (for example, the ray and the catfish), if touched, could send a mysterious and very unpleasant tingling sensation right through a person's body. They even explored the medical possibilities of using such shocks to cure gout and migraine; how successful they were is still a matter for conjecture.

But it was one of the very early Greek philosophers, Thales of Miletus (*c.* 600 BCE), who took the first tentative steps along the road to our understanding of the phenomenon. As a passionate student of nature, he noticed that a strange force was generated when amber (fossilized resin) was vigorously rubbed, and his discovery became the starting point for the seventeenth-century scientists who revisited the mystery. In fact, it was the material they based their observations on that gave us the word 'electricity'; the Ancient Greek for amber was *ēlektron*, a word derived from *ēlektōr*, 'the beaming sun'.

> Communism is Soviet government plus electrification of the whole country.
>
> VLADIMIR LENIN, *Our Foreign and Domestic Position and Early Tasks* (1920)

Engineer

Few engineers would wish to disagree with the assertion that they are all 'geniuses' who display an above-average degree of 'ingenuity', but etymologically speaking the statement is true.

As early as the twelfth century the word 'engineer' was being used with a negative if not pejorative meaning of 'schemer' (the idea survives today when we talk about people who 'engineer' events), but by the mid-fourteenth century an engineer was a man who built complicated weapons of war. It was not until the fifteenth century that the term had acquired the meaning we attach to it in the modern world: an inventor or designer of the complicated pieces of machinery demanded by modern living. The mainly American use of calling engine drivers 'engineers' dates from the 1830s.

'Engineers' take their name from the Old French word *engin*, which meant 'skill' or 'wit', and this in turn was derived from the Latin *ingenium*, a sort of blanket term for inherited talents and innate abilities, related to the Greek *gignesthai*, 'to be born'. And the Indo-European root here is **gen*, the source of dozens of words scattered throughout many European languages which have connections (sometimes rather obscure) with birth or creation. This is not particularly surprising when we remember that an 'engineer' is a 'creative' man or woman who uses his or her 'innate abilities' (the real meaning of 'genius') to create artefacts which previously did not exist. And the less gifted among us are frequently astonished at the 'ingenuity' behind some of their creations.

The Greeks had another word for people who built complicated structures: *mēkhanopoios*, literally 'machine maker', a word directly related to the term we use to define someone skilled in constructing or maintaining appliances and devices, 'mechanic'.

> When a true genius appears in the world you may know him by this sign, that the dunces are all in a confederacy against him.
>
> JONATHAN SWIFT, *Thoughts on Various Subjects* (1706)

Farmer

The meaning of this word has changed dramatically since the fifteenth century. Today, whether he or she specializes in arable, dairy or sheep farming the common denominator is always the same: farmers earn their living from the land and this involves hard work from dawn until dusk, frequently with minimal time off for holidays or rest.

But the word has had this meaning only since the 1590s. When it entered English in the fourteenth century (derived from the Anglo-French *fermer* and Old French *fermier*) it referred to the person whose responsibility it was to collect the taxes or rent from the man who hired the land for tilling or tending his livestock. The Anglo-French and Old French terms were derived from the Medieval Latin *firma*, meaning 'a fixed' or 'firm' payment.

In the Middle Ages and earlier, one of the more normal terms for the man who worked the land in order to feed his family and his community was 'churl', a word which has etymological links spanning the whole spectrum of the social hierarchy.

To the Anglo-Saxons a *ceorl*, as the word was then spelled, was originally just a 'man' or 'husband'. It then came to define the lowest member of a rigidly stratified society, a peasant or serf who, despite being a free man, kept body and soul together by undertaking the most menial tasks. By the thirteenth century the word was synonymous with 'miser', and by the sixteenth it was a pejorative term for anyone who behaved in an unacceptable or boorish manner. And this has given us our modern adjective, 'churlish'.

But the word is also directly connected to the Middle Low German *Kerle*, 'man', the Norse *karl*, 'old man', and the Medieval Latin Christian name *Carolus*, the modern form of which is 'Charles'. In the eighth–ninth centuries a certain Carolus Magnus (742–814) was the king of the Franks; his name is known to us now in its more recognizable form, Charlemagne.

Fettler

In colloquial English, particularly as it is spoken in the northern part of the country, anything or anyone described as being 'in fine fettle' is in tip-top condition and ready to perform whatever duties and tasks lie ahead. And in Lancashire, for instance, if a person says 'I've fettled it' he or she will be informing those close by that whatever the problem was, it has now been solved.

In the wider workplace, a 'fettler' can mean a variety of things depending on the context. On the railways a fettler does the repair work and maintenance on the tracks; in a ceramics factory he or she will be responsible for cleaning off the rough edges on a piece of pottery before it is sent away for firing. In the woollen mills, fettlers still clear any loose or tangled strands of wool from machinery before setting about removing all the filthy grease that might have accumulated on the carding engines, thereby hindering the smooth operation of fabric production.

But the meanings attached to the words 'fettle' and 'fettler' now provide little if any clue to the derivation of the words. In the Middle Ages the verb 'to fettle' had two meanings: it meant 'to prepare oneself' generally for whatever task lay ahead, but it also meant specifically 'to prepare oneself for battle'. And this is an indicator of the word's origin: in Old English a *fetel* meant 'a belt' and was directly related to the German *Fessel*, a 'chain', 'bond' or 'band'. Over the centuries such a 'belt', in a military context, referred to the one to which a scabbard and sword were attached, another name for which was a 'girdle'. So, if we have 'girded up our loins' and are now prepared for whatever lies ahead, we may also say that we have taken up the sword, literally or metaphorically, and are now 'in fine fettle'.

> I'll put a girdle round the earth
> In forty minutes.

> WILLIAM SHAKESPEARE, *A Midsummer
> Night's Dream* (1595–96?), 2.1

Firefighter

Since the very first cavemen found that by rubbing two sticks together they could produce a fire, the dual nature of the phenomenon has been clear: it can be a wonderful source of comforting warmth when kept under control, but devastating in its power when not. Hence even in primitive societies provision would have been made for dealing with unwanted fires, and those first on the scene with buckets of water became the firefighters of the day. But, astonishingly, their organization was purely voluntary, random and haphazard; it was not until the Great Fire of London (1666) that people got their heads together and tried to form a body of men who could be relied on to rush out as soon as the alarm was sounded, rescue people from burning buildings and attempt to put the fire out. But, even more astonishingly, it was not until after the Great Fire of Edinburgh in 1824, when most of the centre of the old town was destroyed, that steps were taken to establish firefighting units resembling those we recognize today.

The word 'fire' is related to the Ancient Greek *pur*, as is another word we use in specific circumstances, 'pyre' and the technical term for the art of firework manufacturing, 'pyrotechnics'. Also, as a testimony to the cleansing properties of the flames, it is possibly closely related to the English 'pure'.

The French for 'fire' is the etymologically related *feu*, which has interesting historical associations. During the Middle Ages, with houses made largely of timber and packed close together, municipal authorities were only too well aware of the constant danger of a disastrous fire. Every evening, bells were tolled in towns and cities throughout the land informing the good citizens that it was time for them to cover (by which they meant 'extinguish') any fires burning in their houses. The Anglo-Norman for this was *coeverfeu* (literally 'cover fire'), which became the modern 'curfew', now used to denote the hours when people have to stay indoors during an emergency.

> The curfew tolls the knell of parting day,
> The lowing herd wind slowly o'er the lea,
> The plowman homewards plods his weary way,
> And leaves the world to darkness and to me.

THOMAS GRAY, 'Elegy Written in a
Country Churchyard' (1751)

Fisherman

Fishing is a skill as old as humankind. We began devising methods of catching fish in order to survive almost as soon as we could walk, and the most successful of these, the rod and line or the net, are still the commonest means of getting fish out of the water and onto dry land.

It was not until the 1520s that a catcher of fish was first defined as a 'fisherman'. Prior to that date he was simply a 'fisher' (hence 'fishers of men' in the King James Bible, 1611), derived from the Old English *fisc*, 'fish', a form of the word which bore a close resemblance to those in other Germanic languages: Old Saxon and Old High German also had *fisc*, Old Norse had *fiskr*, and Gothic had *fisks*. Modern German and Dutch have *Fisch* and *visch* respectively.

By contrast, Latin and the Romance languages have basically the same word but have an initial *p* where Germanic languages have a *f*, so the Latin word was *piscis*, Spanish is *pez* (or *pescado* when it is dead and on the table), and French has the slightly altered form of *poisson*. And this feature of the Latin-based languages shows up in the French and Spanish words for a 'swimming pool', *piscine* and *piscina*, which originally meant 'fish pond'.

Of course, the other term for a fisherman, somewhat archaic but still applied in English to the recreational catcher of fish, is 'angler'. This is a fifteenth-century word based on 'angle', meaning a 'fish hook', with an etymology leading back to the Ancient Greeks. Their word for 'bent' or 'crooked' was *ankulos*, a perfect description of the part of an angler's fishing tackle which originally would probably have been just a bent pin.

> You will find angling to be like the virtue of humility, which has a calmness of spirit and a world of other blessings attending upon it.
>
> IZAAK WALTON, *The Compleat Angler* (1653)

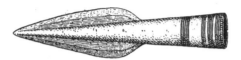

Fletcher

'In days of old, when knights were bold', just about everybody needed the services of a fletcher. Before the invention of firearms, bows and arrows were used in both war and peace, either as a means of destroying the enemy or as an indispensable accoutrement of the hunter. This meant that the man who made arrows for, or sold arrows to, bowmen was able to make a respectable living.

Strictly speaking, however, the derivation of the word tells us that the 'fletcher' was only one of two people involved in the production of arrows. The word 'fletcher' is closely related to the verb 'to fletch', meaning 'to fit feathers onto an arrow', the Germanic root here being **fleug*, 'to fly' (also seen in the modern German for an aeroplane, *Flugzeug*). In other words, the original 'fletcher' was the man who helped arrows 'fly' to their target. In the 1560s another cognate word appeared in English: 'to fledge', meaning 'to acquire feathers and be ready to fly', as in the case of a young bird.

The other person whose skills were in great demand for the production of arrows was the 'arrowsmith'. He was the man who worked on the business end of the arrow, the iron tip, which had to be especially forged and tempered to make it capable of piercing an enemy's armour.

And Arrowsmith, of course, is also a surname. But there is something of a conundrum here. If 'arrowsmiths' and 'fletchers' were both involved in the manufacture of arrows, why is Fletcher a very common surname, but Arrowsmith is very rare? Surely the names should occur with more or less the same frequency?

The answer to the question appears to be the fact that the name Fletcher is not always derived from the occupation of the man who made arrows. Historically it was frequently confused with 'flesher', the man whose job it was to scrape and clean animal skins before they were sent off to be converted into leather.

> To be, or not to be; that is the question:
> Whether 'tis nobler in the mind to suffer
> The slings and arrows of outrageous fortune,
> Or to take arms against a sea of troubles,
> And, by opposing, end them?
>
> WILLIAM SHAKESPEARE, *Hamlet* (1599–1602?), 3.1

Fuller

People with the surname Fuller, Walker or Tucker all have one thing in common: at some point in their ancestry their forebears were involved in the wool trade. Historically, the production of woollen cloth involved a good deal of tramping, or 'fulling', on the raw wool to remove all the dirt and grease; the people who engaged in this task for their living were known usually as 'fullers' but could also be referred to as 'walkers' or 'tuckers'.

In Ancient Rome the custom was to place the wool in a shallow vat of human urine (a prized commodity then with several industrial uses) and then set the *fullones* or 'fullers' tramping all over it until it was smooth and malleable.

The Latin singular noun *fullo*, 'fuller', made its way into Old English, which had *fullere*, and its derivative verb *fullian*, meaning 'to full' cloth and additionally 'to whiten' it. And when we consider that this process meant subjecting the wool to some pretty violent treatment, such as pounding and thumping, it is not surprising that the etymological equivalent in Old French was *fuler*, 'to trample on', 'to injure', 'to maim'.

By the Middle Ages some of the violence had been taken out of the fulling process, and water mills were replacing the more unpleasant traditional methods, although the use of urine continued until 1376. In the mills the cloth was washed over and over again until it was ready for the next stage. At this point the treated cloth was mounted on huge wooden frames known as 'tenters', where it was stretched to the maximum, thus ensuring that it retained a square shape when dry. And the stretching and pulling was achieved by attaching the cloth to special hooks, known as 'tenterhooks', positioned around the frames.

This part of the 'fulling' process explains why, since the sixteenth century, we have metaphorically described ourselves as being 'on tenterhooks' when we feel emotionally stretched to the limit about something that might happen in the immediate future.

Another sixteenth-century development was the arrival of the variant 'foil', meaning 'to frustrate', as in expressions such as 'to foil someone's plans' or 'to foil an attempt'. No doubt this is a metaphorical development of the Old French verb meaning 'to trample on'.

Gaffer

This is a good example of a pure homonym. It exists in modern English not only with two very distinct meanings but also with two very different origins.

The first meaning of the word appeared in the 1580s as a term of respect for elderly men who lived in rural England and no doubt were able to pass on to the younger generation words of wisdom about nature, the seasons and the importance of living in harmony with the environment.

By the early 1840s the word had taken on an additional meaning within the context of the increasing industrialization of the country. It was now applied to men who had been put in charge of a group of workers and were responsible for making sure they carried out their duties efficiently and that the work schedule was adhered to. In other words, a 'gaffer' was now an alternative term for a boss or foreman.

The word 'gaffer' with the above uses is almost certainly derived from the twelfth-century English word 'godfather' (in Anglo-Saxon times this was *godfæder*), who attended baptism ceremonies and vowed to take care of the infant's religious upbringing.

The second 'gaffer' is a very different animal. In a television studio or on a film set, a 'gaffer' is the chief electrician responsible for the lighting; he or she works closely with the producer in deciding how the lighting should match the action in various scenes of the play or film as it progresses.

But there is more to the job than simply knowing which spotlight to turn on at any given time. The gaffer is also in charge of the overhead equipment which allows the lights to move around as different parts of the set need the lighting to be brighter or dimmer. The technical term for this equipment is the 'gaff', a word which was a medieval borrowing of the Middle French *gaffe*, derived from the

Old Occitan *gaf*, 'hook', and the verb *gafer*, 'to seize', 'to grab'. To put it another way, 'gaffer' in a theatrical setting refers to whoever is in charge of the 'hooks' that 'grab hold' of the spotlights.

Gamekeeper

The term 'gamekeeper' has featured in English since the 1660s. It is a title applied to the person responsible for looking after areas of the countryside which provide a habitat for the animals hunted for sport. These 'animals' (a term that includes birds and fish) have been collectively known as 'game' since *c.* 1300 for one simple reason. The people taking part in hunting them considered it a sporting activity or 'game' from which they derived (some might argue dubious) feelings of pleasure and satisfaction.

The term 'game' has many cognates in the Germanic languages, including Swedish *gamman*, Danish *gamen*, Old High German *gaman*, all of which mean 'fun', 'joy', 'merriment', as did the Old English word *gamen*. And the origin of the word is thought by some to lie in the combination of the Proto-Germanic collective prefix **ga*, 'together', and **mann*, 'man', 'person', implying that when people gather together the inevitable result is laughter, merriment and good sport.

Since the early fifteenth century the word 'sport' has conveyed a similar idea. But there is a difference. Etymologically, the word 'game' suggests 'coming together', but with 'sport' the emphasis is on escape. It was originally 'disport', comprising the Latin prefix *dis*, 'away', 'apart', and the verb *portare*, 'to carry', the basic idea here being that when the noun 'disport' was used in English in the fourteenth century, it meant 'frolic', 'pastime', but literally an activity designed to 'carry one away' from the pots and pans of everyday living.

'Sport' did not acquire the meaning 'athletic contest' in English until the sixteenth century.

> I see you stand like greyhounds in the slips,
> Straining upon the start. The game's afoot.
> Follow your spirit, and upon this charge
> Cry, 'God for Harry! England and Saint George!
>
> WILLIAM SHAKESPEARE, *Henry V* (1599), 3.1

Gardener

The man or woman who looks after a cultivated plot of land, either professionally or as an amateur, has been known as a 'gardener' in English since the thirteenth century (the Old English term was *wyrtweard*, literally 'plant guard'). This was about the time when the word 'garden' entered the language from the Old French *jardin*, a borrowing of a Germanic word, cognate with Old English *geard*, pronounced 'yard'. In other words, our 'garden' and 'yard' are essentially the same word.

But the Old English *geard* had a much wider set of meanings than its modern counterpart. It was used to define all or any of: fence, enclosure, region, courtyard and even dwelling.

Perhaps the most important point to notice here is that all the meanings of the Old English word suggest surrounding or fencing off an area of land for a specific purpose. This explains many, if not all, of the cognate nouns in other languages. The Greek *khortos* was a plot of land reserved specifically for feeding cattle; the Latin *hortus* was a garden or park but also gave us the words 'horticulture' and 'orchard'. And another distant relation here is the Russian *górod*, 'town', which shows up in its contracted form, *grad*, in place names such as Volgograd (formerly Stalingrad), Leningrad (now St Petersburg) and Kaliningrad.

And I wove the thing to a random rhyme,
For the Rose is Beauty, the Gardener, Time.

AUSTIN DOBSON, 'A Fancy from Fontanelle' (1904?)

Gongfarmer

Thankfully, this occupation has long since disappeared from the list of possible jobs open to young people considering their future career choices. Modern sewerage systems and domestic plumbing have meant that the gongfarmer is no longer seen going about his business in English towns and villages during the hours of darkness. But in Tudor times he was a common feature of the nocturnal landscape as he removed bucketloads and cartloads of human excrement from the primitive latrines and cesspits dotted around areas of human habitation. And the job was considered so disgusting by the general populace, who did not want to be offended by the sight and smells of the gongfarmers going about their awful business, that they insisted the work be done between the hours of nine at night and five in the morning. Thus the contents of their buckets and carts were euphemistically referred to as 'night soil'.

The word 'gong' could refer to either a latrine ('house of easement' was another term for those 'conveniently' situated in public places) or to the contents themselves. The derivation of the word is the Old English *gangan*, meaning 'to go', leading us to believe that, historically, both the ordure and the place where it was produced took their names from those occasions when honest citizens had to find somewhere private if they suddenly felt the need 'to go'.

PUREFINDER

The gongfarmers were not the only people who, in years gone by, made a less than fragrant living out of gathering up excrement. In London, during the 1840s and 1850s, there were people who earned their crust by roaming the streets and collecting dog mess, which they then sold on to tanning factories where it was used in the transformation of animal hide into leather. They were referred to by the wonderfully euphemistic definition 'purefinders'. By all accounts, the occupation was relatively lucrative and much sought after by those in need of a job.

Grocer

In the modern world a grocer is a man or woman who sells a wide variety of foodstuffs. Those who are a little more specialized in what they offer the public are called 'greengrocers' and they concentrate on selling 'greens' – that is, vegetables and fruit.

When the word entered English, however, in the fifteenth century, it was spelled *grosser* (from the Old French *grossier*) and referred to merchants who sold sugar, dried fruit and spices. And as spices were probably the most important (i.e. profitable) item in which these traders trafficked, they were alternatively referred to as 'spicers', still with us today in the surname 'Spicer'.

The original meaning of the word 'grocer' came not from what was on offer, but from the manner in which the goods were obtained. In the Middle Ages, the Medieval Latin term for a wholesale trader who bought the foodstuffs he intended to sell to retailers in large quantities was *grossarius* (a noun derived from the adjective *grossus*, meaning 'large' or 'bulky'). Then, as now, it was a case of the more the merchant sold, the greater was his profit.

The medieval term *grossarius* was based on the Old French expression *grosse dozeine*, a 'fat dozen', which was the usual quantity in which merchants of the time found it convenient to conduct their trade. More specifically, a *grosse dozeine* was twelve dozen of anything, which explains why we still refer to 144 individual items as twelve dozen or 'a gross'.

God made the wicked Grocer
For a mystery and a sign,
That men might shun the awful shops,
And go to inns to dine

      G.K. CHESTERTON, 'The Song against Grocers' (1914)

Groom

In the British (and formerly English) royal household, the word 'groom' has been applied historically to a number of officials with duties of varying degrees of onerousness and intimacy. Over the centuries, monarchs have employed grooms to carry out many ordinary, everyday tasks, which, theoretically at least, meant that the king or queen could get on with the business of ruling the country. There have been Grooms of the Chamber, Grooms of the Privy Chamber, Grooms of the Robes, to name but a few. Almost certainly the position with the smallest number of applicants, however, was the Groom of the Stool, instituted by Henry VIII and finally discontinued by Edward VII in 1901. This lucky servant of the Crown was expected to attend the monarch at all times and, when he or she had used 'the stool' (a euphemism for the toilet), wash and clean the royal posterior.

Nowadays, away from royal residences, a groom is more likely to be found in stables, looking after the horses, making sure that they are exercised, well fed and kept in good condition.

The word itself has had something of a chequered history. Around the year 1200, *grome*, as it was then spelled, simply meant a 'male child'; a hundred years later it was a term applied to any youth, but could also be the term for a male servant. In royal and noble households at this time, a 'groom' was both a minor official enjoying a position one notch above a page and also a squire attending a knight. His employment as a stable hand dates only from the seventeenth century.

When we turn our attention to the use of the word as in 'bridegroom', things get a little complicated. The Old English term was *brȳdguma* (*guma*, meaning 'man' or 'hero', is related to the Latin for 'man', *homo*); it appears that this word acquired the otherwise unexplained 'r' by contagion, thus producing the modern 'groom'.

Harbinger

The only time we are likely to come across this word in modern English is when somebody, waxing somewhat lyrical, speaks of a 'harbinger of doom' or a 'harbinger of spring', so it is perhaps surprising to discover that the word was originally used to define a job or occupation.

In Old French a *herbergere* was the man who, probably together with his wife, ran an inn offering shelter for the night to weary travellers in the French countryside (modern French still has the related noun *auberge*). But the origins of the word are Germanic; the Old High German *heriberga* comprised two other words, *heri*, 'army', and *berg*, 'protected place', so that the basic idea behind the word was a place where an army, or at least a detachment of soldiers, could shelter in the knowledge that they were reasonably well protected, should an enemy attack during the night.

But at some time in the sixteenth century the meaning changed completely. The noun 'harbinger' was now applied to the man who was detailed to run ahead of an advancing army (or retinue of a monarch or nobleman), to seek out a suitable place for the main party to be fed and provided with a night's lodgings.

> The rest is labour which is not used for you.
> I'll be myself the harbinger, and make joyful
> The hearing of my wife with your approach
>
> WILLIAM SHAKESPEARE, *Macbeth* (1606), 1.4

Hayward

'Hayward' is now encountered in English almost exclusively as a surname, but in the Middle Ages, when the country-dwellers far outnumbered those who lived in towns, 'haywards' were to be found everywhere. When the word was first recorded in English in the thirteenth century, it referred to the men whose job it was to keep the 'hedges' or 'fences' around the fields in good repair. In medieval rural society, cattle straying into a field could have a devastating effect on the crops, with dreadful implications for the local food supply. It was the hayward's job to make sure this did not happen.

The Old English for a hedge or fence was *hecg*, and this combined with the word for a guardian, *weard*, to give *hegeweard*, 'hayward', literally 'the guardian of the hedge' (totally unrelated to 'hay', meaning 'cut and dried grass', which is derived from the verb 'to hew'). The Indo-European root here is *kagh*, frequently found in words associated with containment, such as 'colander', 'cage', 'gaol', and another Old English word, *haga*, 'an enclosure'. This is closely related to *hecg* and is an earlier form of 'haw', recognizable in 'hawthorn', the bush universally regarded as one of the best for making reliable, substantial hedges around fields or enclosures.

The hedge that contains, of course, also protects, which explains why we talk figuratively even today about 'hedge funds' and 'hedging our bets'; both are terms associated with protecting our money, or at least making sure we don't lose more than we can afford.

And there is another surprising association. The Indo-European root also provides the German *Hexe*, a witch, known in English since the thirteenth century as 'hag', an evil female spirit. It is not absolutely clear what the connection here is but it has been suggested that these malevolent women were so-called because they had a habit of sitting astride hedges and perhaps sleeping beneath them. The use of the term to describe a repulsive old woman dates from the fourteenth century.

There's such divinity doth hedge a king
That treason can but peep to what it would

WILLIAM SHAKESPEARE, *Hamlet* (1599–1602?), 4.5

Henchman

We hardly ever use this word today except in a negative, even pejorative, way. We talk, for example, of Hitler's 'henchmen', frequently referring to the SS murder squads who were prepared to commit heinous crimes in the hope of currying favour with the *Führer*. More recently, the word has been used generally to define morally bankrupt toadies who, whatever the context, surrender their integrity in order to ingratiate themselves and gain favour with people of stronger, if repugnant, personalities.

The word was first used with this meaning in 1839. It was originally applied to young men who aspired to the honourable position of 'squire' or 'page of honour', for which it was simply an alternative term.

As far as we know, the word was first used in Anglo-Norman in 1360 and denoted specifically a young man tasked with looking after his master's horse. The term is derived from the Old English *hengest*, meaning 'horse', and in particular 'stallion'. The modern German for stallion is still *Hengst*.

According to the historian the Venerable Bede (673 CE–735 CE), Hengist and his brother Horsa (whose name is also derived from a word for 'horse') led an invading army, comprising Jutes, Saxons and Angles, from the area of Europe we now think of as Denmark and northern Germany, in the fifth century CE, landing at Ebbsfleet on Kent's east coast. Horsa was killed by the Ancient Britons a few years later, but his brother went on to become king of Kent and to found a dynasty which ruled the county and gave it its unique character among the other counties of Britain. Even today, Kent is known as the 'Invicta' county because it was never beaten into submission, but arrived at an understanding with William of Normandy in 1066, when the rest of the country was subdued by force.

> I speak Spanish to God, Italian to women,
> French to men and German to my horse.
>> CHARLES V, Holy Roman Emperor (1500–1558), attr.

Horologist

Early civilizations used the heavens to account for the passage of the hours; the modern English 'moon' is derived from the Indo-European root *me- (the same root that gave us 'measure'), and the earliest known sundial, dating back to 1500 BCE, was discovered in the Valley of the Kings in Egypt. When we then turned to more terrestrial means of time measurement we devised various contraptions including water clocks, hour- (or sand-) glasses (remember the 'sands of time'?), adapted oil lamps and even calibrated candles.

Mechanical clocks made their appearance in Europe in the early fourteenth century; although they were not very accurate and rather cumbersome, they probably marked the beginning of clockmaking as we know it today. In 1656 the very first pendulum clock was invented in Holland by the Dutch scientist Christiaan Huygens (1629–1695), and later on in the same century the first pocket watch, as we would recognize it, was invented. Whereas this had the advantage of at least being portable, it was far from accurate or reliable, and it was not until the arrival of the first balance springs a few years later that people could look forward to being able to tell the time with a reasonable degree of confidence. But Huygens's pendulum clock remained the most reliable of all until the 1930s.

'Horologist', synonymous with 'watchmaker' or 'clockmaker', is based on the French word *horologue* and entered English in the fourteenth century. This was derived from the Latin *horologium*, meaning both a sundial and a water clock, and the Greek *horologion*, a device for measuring the passage of time or the hours (Greek *hora*, 'hour', 'time').

> Love's not Time's fool, though rosy lips and cheeks
> Within his bending sickle's compass come;
> Love alters not with his brief hours and weeks,
> But bears it out even to the edge of doom.
>
> WILLIAM SHAKESPEARE, Sonnet 116 (1609)

Illustrator

Illustrators are usually artists who are employed to produce drawings which will be included alongside written text, either to clarify and support what has been written, or to make the text easier to understand. On the other hand, comics, graphic novels, greeting cards frequently include the work of illustrators when the consumer prefers to be informed or entertained by visual images rather than a lengthy text. And if, using slightly old-fashioned jargon, we gaze in wonder at an illustrator's work and decide that it is 'devilishly' good, we are closer to the word's historical connections than we perhaps realize.

When the word was first used in English in the sixteenth century, the verb 'to illustrate' simply meant 'to explain', 'to throw light on', whatever subject was under discussion and needed a little extra clarification. It was not until the 1630s that the verb acquired the additional meaning of 'to provide explanatory pictures'. And anyone who drew attractive little drawings or pictures has been referred to as an 'illustrator' only since the 1680s.

The derivative Latin verb was *illustrare*, a compound of *lustrare*, meaning 'to illuminate'. This verb was itself a derivative of *lustrere*, 'to make bright', 'to shine light upon', from the verb *lucere*, 'to shine', 'to be bright', which had the associated noun *lux*, 'light'.

This is where things get even more interesting. By combining the noun *lux* with the verb *ferre*, 'to bring', we arrive at the noun *lucifer*, meaning literally 'the bringer of light'. In Roman mythology, Lucifer was the personification of the morning star rising above the horizon at dawn and bathing the world in daylight. But there is a problem here as Lucifer is also a name by which the Devil is known in Christianity. So how did the Devil (also termed the Prince of Darkness) acquire an epithet describing him as the one who brings light into the world? It appears that St Jerome (*c.* 347–420) and other early Christian writers came across the term 'Lucifer' when translating the Bible from Greek and Hebrew into Latin, and mistakenly thought it was an allusion to the Devil; in fact it was a rather flattering, even sycophantic, reference to an unidentified king of Babylon.

> Unhappy spirits that fell with Lucifer,
> Conspired against our God with Lucifer,
> And are forever damned with Lucifer.
>
> CHRISTOPHER MARLOWE, *Doctor Faustus* (1592), 1.3

Infantryman

Two English words that conjure up very different, and probably totally conflicting, images are 'infantryman' and 'infant'. The former makes us think of a battle-hardened, resilient soldier slogging his way through hostile territory, often facing a hail of shells and bullets, as he attempts to drive back a valiant foe, forcing him to flee, surrender or be killed. The latter evokes the sight of a helpless, nappy-clad, newly born item of humanity who is totally dependent on adults for his or her sustenance and very existence. And yet these two vastly contrasting images are, etymologically speaking, inextricably linked.

In the 1570s it became common practice to refer to foot soldiers as the 'infantry'; whereas it had been usual to talk about 'regiments of foot' and so on, the Italian or Spanish designation *infanteria* (via the French *infanterie*) became the preferred term in England also. In Italy and Spain the *infanteria* were the young fighting men who were thought of as being far too inexperienced (or of too lowly birth) to be allowed to join the cavalry.

And the key word here is 'young'. By the time the word 'infantry' was being applied to the young men who fought on the battlefields of Europe, it had changed quite a bit in meaning. It was now virtually synonymous with the phrase 'young fighting men'; but its original meaning was very different.

The original Latin word was *infans*, comprising *in*, 'not', and *fans*, 'speaking' (from the infinitive *fari*, 'to speak'), used to describe a newborn child who had still not acquired the ability to communicate using language.

So runs my dream: but what am I?
  An infant crying in the night:
  An infant crying for the light:
And with no language but a cry.

ALFRED, LORD TENNYSON, In Memoriam (1850)

Janitor

The handyman or caretaker who looks after a building, doing small repairs and making sure the working environment is clean, tidy and safe for those who need to be there, is sometimes referred to as a 'janitor'. In the 1580s the term was used in England to describe an 'usher' or assistant teacher in a school, but by the 1620s his duties had been reduced to those of a doorkeeper. By about 1700 his allotted tasks had expanded again to include the general upkeep of the building, much the same as they do today.

The word 'doorkeeper' is the key to the etymology of the word. In Ancient Rome the *janitor* was the man who opened and closed the *janua* or main door of a building as visitors came and went. And to the Ancient Romans such a responsible position was personified in the form of a deity, *Janus*, the god of comings and goings, beginnings and endings, and of doors, arcades and entrances. He was always depicted as a tutelary god with two faces, simultaneously looking in opposite directions, just as a door can open inwards and outwards.

Symbolically, such a deity was perfectly suited to representing the first month of the year as it was a time when people could look forward to the new year, but could still look back at the events of the previous one. A god facing the future but still looking into the past was also the perfect choice for the Romans when they called the first month *Januarius mensis*, 'Janus's month'. In thirteenth-century England this evolved into 'January', replacing the Old English expression *æftera Gēola*, literally meaning the month 'after Yule' (or Christmas).

Latin also had another word for gate or door, *porta*. This produced the Late Latin noun *portarius*, also meaning 'doorkeeper', which by the thirteenth century had become 'porter' in English, a synonym for 'janitor'.

> Pale Death with impartial foot knocks at the doors
> of poor men's hovels and of kings' palaces.
>
> HORACE, *Odes* (*c.* 23 BCE)

Jeweller

The professional jeweller takes his or her name from the jewellery he or she creates or sells in shops that have adorned our high streets for centuries. We cannot be absolutely sure when men (and women) were first seduced by the charms of gold, silver and precious stones, but we do know that as far back as 1600 BCE the Ancient Greeks were using such items for personal adornment. A century later they had learned the basic techniques of the goldsmith's art and appreciated the beauty of emeralds, diamonds, rubies and many more of the precious stones known to us today.

Throughout the ages jewellery of all sorts has held a fatal fascination for people all over the world; men have fought over it, killed for it and died for it. In fact, its acquisition has always been a 'deadly' serious matter and nothing to laugh or joke about, which is rather odd when we come to look at the derivation of the word.

The first use of the term 'jeweller' in English was in the fourteenth century; it was a derivative of 'jewel', a word which entered English in the thirteenth century. But this word is a descendant of the Old French *joel* (modern French *jeu*) and the Latin *jocus*, meaning 'jest', 'joke' and 'game'.

Looking at the linguistic evidence, then, we might conclude that the chunks of minerals modern men and women often spend vast amounts of money on were once considered little more than toys or playthings used to bring a little enjoyment and amusement into the lives of the ordinary people.

> Bonnie wee thing, cannie wee thing,
> Lovely wee thing, wert thou mine,
> I wad wear thee in my bosom
> Lest my jewel I would tine.*

ROBERT BURNS, 'The Bonnie Wee Thing' (1791)

---

* 'Tine' is a Scots word meaning 'to lose'.

Journalist

In the modern world there are many kinds of journalist: financial, legal, sporting, investigative, and so on. They all play important roles in our lives as they inform us, entertain us and, in some cases, attempt to persuade us to support a political party or to side with the paper over a burning issue of the day. But whatever their political persuasion, no matter how convincingly they write or how well they perform in front of the cameras, all journalists take their job title from the same etymological source.

In the eighteenth century the word 'journal' was used for the first time to denote a daily newspaper, although the term 'journalist' had been in use since the seventeenth. A century earlier 'journal' was a term for a daily record of transactions and events, in much the same way that we would think of a diary today. And in the fourteenth century a journal (alternatively spelled 'diurnal') was a list of the appointed times of the day when those who cared about such things were expected to pray.

Whatever historical context the word was used in, the etymology remained the same: it is derived from the Old French *jurnel*, which was derived from the Latin *diurnum*, 'an account book', 'a daily allowance'. And the Latin roots here are, of course, *diurnus*, 'pertaining to the day', and the noun *dies*, 'day'.

Since 1882 there has been another kind of journalist: the 'freelance'. This is a description that harks back to the days of yore when knights fought for their lords and protected fair damsels. Some of them chose not to be tied to a particular lord but were 'free' to hire out their 'lances' to whoever was willing to pay.

Although the medieval mercenary soldiers operated on a 'freelance' basis, the term did not appear until the nineteenth century. It is generally accepted that it was coined by Sir Walter Scott (1771–1832) in his novel of knights of old, *Ivanhoe*, published in 1819, but there are those who point out that the term had been used as early as 1809 by Thomas Brown in his novel *The Life and Times of Hugh Miller.*

Journeyman

This is (very understandably) a much misunderstood word; the temptation is to assume that it has something to do with travel, which it has, but not in the way many people assume.

In the Middle Ages it was the custom for labourers and artisans to work for a master or employer on a minimum contract of three months, but frequently this was extended to a year. And the law was firmly on the side of the employer. If a labourer decided that he did not like working where he was or had the offer of a better placement, he did not have the right to terminate his original agreement and just leave. The result was that a goodly number of artisans simply refused to enter into any agreement at all and offered their services, wherever and to whomsoever, they wished. Many preferred the freedom of working for, and being paid by, the day – and this leads us to the derivation of the word. The Old French word *journée* (from *jour*, 'day') meant 'amount accomplished in a day', 'a day's work', and this, combined with 'man', found its way into English in the fourteenth century as 'journeyman'.

The reason for the confusion with travel is quite simple. We now think of a 'journey' as a distance covered by travel, irrespective of the time taken to complete it. The original meaning, however, was 'the distance covered in a day'.

> Does the road wind up-hill all the way?
>   Yes, to the very end.
> Will the day's journey take the whole long day?
>   From morn to night, my friend.
>
> CHRISTINA ROSSETTI, *Up-Hill* (1861)

Judge

Most of us probably think of a judge as the man wearing a large, anachronistic wig, sitting behind an enormous desk and surveying an assembly of people in a court of law. And his responsibility, of course, is to preside over the proceedings, making sure that they conform to the law of the land and that whoever stands in the dock is given a fair trial.

The term entered English at some time around the year 1200 and was a borrowing of the Old French *juge* and the verb *jugier*, 'to make a diagnosis', 'to judge'. This was derived from the Latin verb *judicare*, 'to examine officially', and the noun *judex*, 'judge'. The modern spelling with -dg- did not appear in English until the middle of the fifteenth century.

But *judex* was a combination of two other Latin words: *jus*, 'law', and *dicere*, 'to say'. That is, our word 'judge' is derived from Latin roots meaning essentially 'one who speaks on matters concerning the law'.

When the Normans took over the legal system in what had been Anglo-Saxon England, they imposed their legal terminology on the indigenous population, along with a new set of laws. Prior to their arrival, the Old English for the official who pronounced in matters involving the law was *demend*, derived from another noun, *dom*, 'law' or 'judgement'. This explains why we now have two expressions for what is supposed to happen when we all meet our maker: the 'Day of Judgement' or 'Doomsday', the more recognizable form of the Old English *dōmes dæg*.

The modern sense of the word 'doom', with all its negative connotations of chaos, death and destruction, dates only from the early fourteenth century.

Give every man thine ear but few thy voice.
Take each man's censure, but reserve thy judgement.
WILLIAM SHAKESPEARE, *Hamlet* (1599–1602), 1.3

Juggler

Most of us, when we hear the word 'juggler', think of an entertainer standing on a stage or in a circus arena throwing assorted objects in the air, catching them and throwing them upwards again. Usually to the admiration and astonishment of the onlookers the juggler manages to propel the objects skywards, control them and keep them airborne until deciding when to terminate the performance. But the dictionary tells us that, in twelfth-century England, a 'juggler' was all of: jester, buffoon, magician, wizard, storyteller and conjuror. The truth is that the profession of 'juggler' has gone through many incarnations over the centuries; it was not until the late nineteenth century that the meaning of the word was confined to manual dexterity and flying objects.

In Middle English the itinerant showman was known as a *jogleor*, a word taken from the Old French *j(o)ulere*, a variant of the *jongleur* (from the verb *jongler*, 'to entertain') who travelled about twelfth-century France entertaining people from all walks of life and strata of society. He would put on a performance in castles, in marketplaces and even in abbeys to bring a little cheer to people's lives on public holidays. But he also had another vital role to play. In a world of almost universal illiteracy and poor communications, the itinerant juggler was frequently the person who brought news of events in other parts of the country, if not the whole of Europe.

The juggler and the *jongleur* both derive their names from Ancient Rome, where the word *ioculator* was somebody who made people laugh, and a *iocus* was the means by which this was achieved. And these two Latin words gave us our 'joker' and 'joke'.

> They brought one Pinch, a hungry lean-faced villain,
> A mere anatomy, a mountebank,
> A threadbare juggler, and a fortune-teller,
> A needy, hollow-eyed, sharp-looking wretch,
> A living dead man.

WILLIAM SHAKESPEARE, *The Comedy of Errors*
(1589–94), 5.1

Knacker

If we describe somebody, perhaps jocularly, as being ready for the 'knacker's yard' we are suggesting that they are past their usefulness and that their best days are well and truly behind them.

The rather graphic description of the sorry state someone might find themselves in, as their former vim and vigour fade, dates from 1812 when the word 'knacker' was first applied to a man whose livelihood consisted at least partly in slaughtering old and sickly horses. Earlier, in the sixteenth century, the 'knacker' (or 'nacker' as it was also spelled) was employed mainly as a maker of saddles and harnesses, but his general association with horses meant that he gradually 'branched out' to help farmers and country-dwellers in general with all equine problems. This eventually included the disposal of dead horses and cattle as well as other farm animals.

The derivation of the word is somewhat problematical, and there appears to be no consensus of opinion among etymologists. All that they seem to agree on is that there is a strong connection with the Old Norse *hnakkur*, meaning 'saddle' and, by extension, the harness and trappings. It is also pointed out that *hnakkur* is connected with another Old Norse word, *hnakki*, 'the back of the neck', and closely linked etymologically with the English 'neck'.

Since 1883 the derivative adjective 'knackered' has been used as a synonym for 'tired out', 'exhausted', or, when applied to inanimate objects, to signify that a car, lawnmower, toaster or kettle is no longer fit for purpose and should be discarded forthwith.

> A horse! A horse! My kingdom for a horse!
> WILLIAM SHAKESPEARE, *Richard III* (1592–93), 5.7

Labourer

Unsurprisingly, a 'labourer' is usually, but not exclusively, a man who 'labours' or works at a physically demanding job. The work is frequently described as being 'unskilled' because no qualifications, and little training, are prerequisites for being taken on. Digging trenches, carrying bricks and clearing drains require energy and muscle-power, not pieces of paper testifying to how many hours' study have been completed.

'Labourer', first used in English in the fourteenth century, was based on the word 'labour', which had entered the language in the thirteenth. Both words can trace their origins back to the Latin noun *labor*, 'exertion', 'suffering' or 'trouble', and its derivative verb, *laborare*, 'to work'. It is also perhaps connected with two other Latin verbs, *labi*, 'to slip', 'to fall down', and *labare*, 'to totter', suggesting that the original idea of 'labouring' included the possibility that anyone so engaged ran the risk of tottering and falling under the weight of a heavy burden.

The Old English equivalent of the Latin-based *labour* was *we(o)rc*, a word with a fascinating linguistic history. It is cognate with the Ancient Greek *ergon*, 'work', which features in our word 'energy', 'the work we have within us', and the 'erg', used to define a unit of work. But, if we go as far back as far as the days of Archaic Greek (*c.* 800 BCE), we find that the Homeric word was *wergon*, beginning with the *w* sound, lost in Ancient Greek but restored by the time it was absorbed into Old English. So the jobs performed by today's 'factory worker' and 'agricultural worker' both have etymological roots reaching back to classical antiquity.

> Which of us, in brief word, is to do the hard and dirty work for the rest of us – and for what pay? Who is to do the pleasant and clean work, and for what pay?
>
> JOHN RUSKIN, *Sesame and Lilies* (1865)

Lawyer

In Anglo-Saxon England the 'law' – that is, a set of rules to which people were expected to adhere so that society could exist and not slide into anarchy – was known as *ǣ*. This was derived from an ancient Germanic root thought to have meant 'the manner', 'the custom' or even 'the way' – the last suggesting that correct behaviour was equated in those days with travelling along a road and keeping to the straight and narrow. Such an interpretation is supported by the fact that *ǣ* was also the term for 'God's law'.

In later Anglo-Saxon times a new word was adopted to define what was considered acceptable conduct, *lagu*, grammatically the plural form of *lag*, which basically referred to anything that had been 'laid down', and is, in fact, a noun related to the modern verb 'to lay'. A 'law', therefore, is simply a rule or regulation that has been 'laid down' for people to acquaint themselves with and then obey.

But a 'lawyer', someone whose profession involves studying the law and explaining it to those who are ignorant of it, was only defined as such in the fourteenth century.

Perhaps surprisingly, the adjective 'legal' is not connected etymologically to the word 'law'. It is derived from the Latin *lex* (genitive *legis*) and only entered English in the 1640s. Its derivative verb is probably the

Latin *legere*, 'to collect', 'to gather', suggesting that, in a nutshell, the noun tells us which rules have been 'laid down' and the adjective tells us which rules have been 'gathered up'.

> The first thing we do let's kill all the lawyers.
> WILLIAM SHAKESPEARE, *2 Henry VI* (*c.* 1591), 4.2

Librarian

Librarians work in libraries and spend their days curating collections of books, magazines, journals and preserving documents for posterity. Another way of putting it would be to say that physically and etymologically they are surrounded by trees. Physically, we all know that books are made of paper and that paper comes ultimately from trees. But there is an etymological dynamic here also in that most of the basic words we (and speakers of other languages) use to define reading material come originally from the magnificent forests that used to cover most of Europe. The basic word 'book', for example, comes originally from the Old English *bōc*, which for the Anglo-Saxons was a document or charter; it was not until the Middle Ages that it came to refer to pages that had been bound together.

But 'book', or *bōc*, as well as the Dutch *boek* and the German *Buch*, are all thought by many etymologists to be related to the German *Buche*, meaning 'beech tree'. The reason is quite simple: in ancient times the bark of the ubiquitous beech tree provided a primitive kind of paper.

If we now consider the derivation of the words 'library' and 'librarian' we find a remarkably similar story. A librarian has acted as the keeper of a library only since 1713, as previously the title referred to a scribe or person who produced handwritten copies of existing books. The term 'library' was a borrowing of the Old French *librairie*, which referred either to a collection of books or to a shop where books were sold (modern French still has *librairie* for 'bookshop'), the double meaning stemming from the original Latin, which had *librarium* for a 'chest of books' and *libraria* for a bookshop. And the derivation of both terms was *liber*, which came to mean 'book' but was originally the Romans' term for the inner bark of a tree.

In many parts of the world it would be a very rare library that did not have at least one version of the Bible on its shelves. And here again a look at the etymology takes us back to primitive writing methods and the ancient forests. 'Bible' is derived from *biblos*, a word used by the Ancient Greeks to refer to a scroll or Egyptian papyrus. But this too was a secondary meaning; the primary meaning of *biblos* was also 'inner bark of a tree'.

Limner

The only time most of us will come across this word is when we visit a museum or some such establishment and gaze in admiration at the beautifully illuminated manuscripts produced by monks in the Middle Ages. Those who demonstrated a talent for art sat from dawn till dusk, day after day, in the monastery scriptorium, producing highly ornate religious texts, many of which have survived to the present day. These gifted individuals were originally known as 'luminers', but by the fourteenth century they were being referred to by the contracted form 'limners'.

The noun is taken from the archaic verb 'to limn', which in the sixteenth century was a synonym for 'to depict', but its derivation was the Middle English *luminen*, which meant specifically 'to illuminate a manuscript'. And *luminen* was derived from the Old French *luminer,* 'to lighten', from the Latin *lumen*, 'light', closely linked to another noun, *luminare*, meaning 'a window', an architectural device for letting light into a building.

The practice of decorating the pages of a book was not confined for ever to those who dwelt within the hallowed walls of a monastery or nunnery (nuns were later involved in the art form as well). By the eighteenth century, secular books were being produced with highly complex designs filling the margins of a printed page; a very common choice, for example, was the vine. Artists worked at producing increasingly complicated convolutions of tendrils trailing around the page margins, particularly on pages featuring drawings or illustrations.

Such intricate depictions of vine tendrils and leaves came to be referred to by the French term *vignettes* (from the French for vine, *vigne*). By 1853 the sense of the word had been transferred to the illustrations themselves. In 1880 'vignette' was first recorded as meaning a brief account of an event or a literary sketch, the meaning we frequently attach to it today.

Ah! Must –
Designer Infinite! –
Ah! must Thou char the wood Ere Thou canst limn with it?

FRANCIS THOMPSON, 'The Hound of Heaven' (1890–92)

Luthier

Apart from those clever people who compile crosswords either for fun or for a living, few people other than professional musicians will be acquainted with this word. On the other hand, anyone who has ever lifted or played a violin, lute or guitar will have touched the product of a 'luthier'.

Originally the word described a person who made or repaired lutes, but by the time the word entered English in the late nineteenth century it was being applied to any craftsperson who specialized in making stringed instruments. It was not used, however, of piano or harp makers as these are constructed by using large wooden frames, which involves an entirely different skill set.

The derivation of the word is the French *luth*, a borrowing of the Old Provençal *laut*, which arrived in Europe in the late thirteenth century from North Africa. And the original Arabic from which *laut* is derived was *al-'ud*, meaning nothing more than 'the wood'. Why such a melodious instrument should simply be referred to as 'the wood' is still the subject of some debate among musicologists and etymologists. Some think it is a reference to the wooden plectrum sometimes used when the instrument is being used; some think it is a reference to the long wooden neck; and yet others see it as referring to the difference between this instrument and similar ones which had animal skins as part of their basic construction. Whatever the truth, it is a musical instrument with a long history and worldwide provenance. Variations of the lute are known to have been played in Ancient Greece, China and India; the earliest form is thought to have existed in Mesopotamia as long ago as 3100 BCE.

> When the lamp is shattered
> The light in the dust lies dead –
> When the cloud is scattered
> The rainbow's glory is shed.
> When the lute is broken,
> Sweet tones are remembered not;
> When the lips have spoken,
> Loved accents are soon forgot.

PERCY BYSSHE SHELLEY, 'Lines' (1824)

Magician

When we watch a magician performing we know it's all illusion, that we are being deceived and that there is probably a simple explanation, but we just can't see it. The man or woman standing in front of us, apparently manipulating the laws of physics, convinces us that we are seeing things which we cannot possibly be seeing, at the same time as making sure that we do not see the hand movements they do not want us to see. With enviable skill, magicians can make things appear out of nowhere, and conversely disappear in a way which our mind tells us is totally impossible. In brief, we constantly (and repeatedly) fall for the same tricks that have baffled onlookers for generations.

The word 'magician' has been around in English since the late fourteenth century, when it made its way into the language from the Old French *magicien*, which in turn was a borrowing from the Late Latin *magice*, a word taken from the Greek *hē magikē tekhnē* (literally 'the art of the Magi'), which has clear biblical connections. The 'wise men' who came from the east bearing gifts for the infant Jesus are alternatively referred to as the Magi, an Old Persian word for members of the educated, priestly class credited with supernatural powers (the Indo-European root *magh* meant 'power').

At some point after the word 'magician' entered English, it replaced the Old English for 'wizard', *drȳ*, etymologically linked to the Irish *drui* and another Celtic word, *druid*, which we still find today in modern English. And all of these are closely linked to the Old English *trēow*, meaning 'tree'. However, there is another twist to the tale. To the Anglo-Saxons there was something 'magical' about trees (especially oak trees) and they viewed them as such powerful symbols of reliability and constancy that *trēow* also came to mean 'trust', 'fidelity' or 'the truth'. This, of course, begs the question for us even today: when we watch a dexterous magician pulling rabbits out of a hat, can we 'trust' what our eyes are telling us, or is what we are witnessing simply a gross distortion of 'the truth'?

||||||||||||||||||||||||||||||||||||||||||||||||||||||||||||||||||||||||||||||||||||||||||||

Dozens of words of Old Persian origin have found their way into English, including, with their literal translations:

Paradise	'walled garden'
Khaki	'dust coloured'
Caravan	'line of camels'
Pagoda	'dwelling for idols'
Turban	'tied up'
Caviar	'Egg bearing'
Shawl	English spelling of *shāl*
Divan	'place of assembly'
Bazaar	'market'
Pyjama	'feet garment'
Tandoori	'oven', 'portable furnace'
Spinach	English spelling of *aspanakh*
Mummy	'wax'
Taffeta	'woven'

||||||||||||||||||||||||||||||||||||||||||||||||||||||||||||||||||||||||||||||||||||||||||||

Manager

Managers who say that they prefer a 'hands on' approach to their job are closer to the derivation of the word than they probably realize. The root of the word is the Latin *manus*, 'hand', which means that 'manager' is cognate with words such as 'manipulate', 'manufacture', 'manicure' and even 'manure' (originally a verb meaning 'to work the land by hand').

When the verb 'to manage' entered English in the sixteenth century it was used almost exclusively in an equestrian context and concerned the breaking-in and training of horses. Its antecedent was the Italian *maneggiare*, 'to control', but again the word's primary sense was of making a horse submit to the will of its trainer. The French version of the word, *manège*, is still used in English with the meaning of a riding school or to define the movements made by a trained horse.

As the verb 'to manage' acquired a more widely spread usage, horses largely dropped out of the equation, so that by 1705 'manager' was an increasingly common designation for the person whose responsibility it was to ensure the smooth running of a business or public institution.

In the twentieth century the term 'project manager' was coined to define a team leader within a company charged with seeing a particular plan through all the stages from conception to completion. Linguistically a project manager took the first word of his or her title ultimately from the Latin verb *proicere*, 'to throw ahead', which itself is made up of *pro*, 'in front of', 'ahead of', and *iacere*, 'to throw'. The past participle *proiectum* meant 'something thrown ahead' and this provided us with the noun we have today, 'project', a plan or idea which has been 'put forward' or 'thrown in front of us' and which now has to be successfully completed.

Mathematician

A Cambridge University Wrangler, struggling with the challenge posed by a complex theorem, and the shopper adding up his or her change at the supermarket checkout have something in common: they are both using mathematics. (A Wrangler is a First-Class Honours graduate in mathematics at the University of Cambridge.) The former might adopt an approach which appears breathtakingly sophisticated to most of us, whereas the latter's will probably be simple addition and subtraction, but the inescapable fact is that they are both using techniques of calculation developed over centuries.

Archaeological evidence has shown that 20,000 years ago there were people in Africa who were attempting basic methods of counting. We have geometrical drawings from Egypt dating back to 5000 BCE, and we know that the Sumerians and Babylonians were using multiplication tables and dealing with the problems of division as far back as 2500 BCE.

But it has to be said that the people who made the greatest contribution to the science of mathematics in Europe were the Greeks. Early philosophers who concerned themselves also with mathematical calculations include Thales (*c.* 624–*c.* 546 BCE), Pythagoras (*c.* 582–*c.* 507 BCE), Archimedes (*c.* 287–212 BCE) and the 'Father of Geometry', Euclid, who was born in the mid-fourth and died in the mid-third century BCE.

The activity which united all these early thinkers has been known in English since the sixteenth century as 'mathematics' and practitioners as 'mathematicians'. Both terms are derived from the Greek *manthanein*, 'to learn', and its derivative plural noun *ta mathēmatika*, literally 'those things that have been learned'.

And, of course, virtually all mathematical activity involves calculation. In its most primitive form, calculation meant counting out little stones or pebbles – and this is a clue to the derivation of the word. The Latin for 'pebble' was *calculus*, cognate with the Greek *khaliks*, also meaning a pebble and probably a reference to the counting stones on an abacus frame. And this adds another dimension to the discussion on mathematics. The word 'abacus' derives from a Semitic root meaning 'dust' or 'sand', reminding us that the most primitive form of counting consisted of making scratch marks in the sand.

Many of the words used today by mathematicians have Greek derivations and include:

Trigonometry	'measurement of triangles' (*trigōnometria*)
Angle	'bent' (*ankulos*)
Geometry	'measurement of the earth' (*gēometria*)
Arithmetic	'counting' (*arithmētikē*)
Isosceles	'equal legs' (*isoskelēs*)
Hypotenuse	'stretched', 'subtending' (*hupoteinousa*)
Theorem	'speculation' (*theorēma*)

An exception here, derived from the Arabic, is:

Algebra	'reunion of broken parts' (*al-jebr*)

Merchant

Almost anybody involved in commerce or trade of any kind can be referred to as a 'merchant', a word which entered English in the thirteenth century. It was borrowed from the French *marchant*, a word derived from the Latin verb *mercari*, 'to trade', and the noun *merx*, 'merchandise'. In modern English we still have a number of words, all associated with commerce, that have come down to us from the same Latin roots: mercenary (concerned with monetary reward), mercantile, mercer (trader in silks and textiles) and, of course, 'market'.

'Market' has since the thirteenth century described the place where people come together to trade and to socialize. But the crowds that gathered on market days frequently gave ample opportunity for the less law-abiding members of the community to find themselves in trouble with the authorities, who from the Middle Ages onwards were allowed by the Crown to set up piepowder courts. These were special courts, established to try vagabonds and thieves who had come to the market from far afield to get up to mischief. As they had almost certainly walked to the market their shoes would have been covered in dirt and dust, and the Anglo-French for 'dusty feet' was *pieds poudrés*. To uneducated anglophone ears this sounded more like 'piepowder'.

There is also believed to be an etymological link with *Mercurius*, known to us as Mercury, the Roman god of tradesmen, marketeers and just about anyone involved in making a profit. Disconcertingly, however, the Romans viewed the same god as the protector of thieves – a cynic might suggest that this demonstrated a less than flattering opinion of those who traded for a living.

Roman gods were, by all accounts, pretty good at multitasking, and in addition to his other duties Mercury was the messenger of the gods. It is this role as a conveyor of news which explains why *The Mercury* has always been a popular title for a newspaper.

Meteorologist

There was a time, within living memory, when the weather was just what you saw when you got out of bed in the morning and drew back the curtains. In summer the sun shone; in winter it rained, snowed or left everything outside covered with frost. Nowadays it is not so simple, and it is becoming quite 'normal' for the meteorological conditions to be 'abnormal for this time of year'.

It is not only the weather that seems to be changing but also the word itself. We can now talk about 'fine weather' or 'dreadful weather', but in the twelfth century 'weather' meant only 'bad weather', and by the fourteenth century the word referred to the direction of the wind. Interestingly, the modern German for weather is the cognate *Wetter*, but another cognate is *véter*, the Russian for wind.

In the modern world, if we are concerned about what the weather is going to be like tomorrow or next week, we turn on the television (or consult a weather app on our phone) and listen to what the meteorologist is saying. And is the relationship between this lady or gentleman and 'meteors' more imagined than real? No; there is in fact a very close connection.

The word 'meteorologist' was first used in English in the early seventeenth century; it was based on the Modern Latin *meteorum*, 'atmosphere', a borrowing from the Ancient Greek *meteōron*, with the same meaning. The Modern Latin and Ancient Greek words were derived from the Greek *metairein*, 'to lift up high', and its derivative noun *ta meteōra*, 'those things lifted up high'. So another Greek word, *meteorologos*, literally meant 'he who studies those things high up' – that is to say, the moon, the sun, the stars and, of course, 'meteors'.

For the early Greek scientists studying the heavenly bodies, it was only a short step to attempting to connect what they saw above with the meteorological conditions they were experiencing below.

> This is the weather the cuckoo likes,
>   And so do I;
> When showers betumble the chestnut spikes,
>   And nestlings fly:
> And the little brown nightingale bills his best,
> And they sit outside at 'The Travellers' Rest'
>
> THOMAS HARDY, 'Weathers' (1913?)

Midwife

Prior to the fourteenth century there was no specific term in English for a woman who helped bring new life into the world. Then the word 'midwife' appeared, combining two others, 'mid' and 'wife'. The first element needs no explanation other than to say that it is simply the Old English *mid*, meaning 'with', but 'wife' did not at the time necessarily imply a 'married woman' as it does today. Any adult female, single or married, could be referred to as a *wīf*, and we still have examples of the word used with its older meaning in modern English. A woman who guts or sells fish for a living is a 'fishwife' and many stories that have been told through the generations are still referred to as 'old wives [i.e. women's] tales'. And 'housewife' in former times described the woman who ran the household, irrespective of whether she was married or a widow or a spinster.

The compound noun 'midwife', therefore, simply denoted a 'woman', whatever her marital status, who was 'with' the mother-to-be as she was about to give birth.

In Anglo-Saxon England the word *wīf* or *wyf* was also combined with another noun we recognize today: man. But 'man' in this context meant a 'human being' of either sex, and so the resulting combination, *wīfman,* defined 'a human being of the female gender'. This evolved into the modern English 'woman'.

Old English had, in fact, two words for 'woman', *wīf* and *cwēn* (often rendered as *quean*), a word that has experienced several dramatic changes of meaning. In Old English it already meant 'woman' (including some fairly pejorative implications) or the 'wife' of a prominent member of society. Eventually it appeared as 'queen' and its application was restricted to the wife of a king.

> O! then I see Queen Mab hath been with you. …
> She is the fairies' midwife, and she comes
> In shape no bigger than an agate stone
> On the forefinger of an alderman
>
> WILLIAM SHAKESPEARE, *Romeo and Juliet* (1597), 1.4

Miller

'Miller' has been around for a long time, both as a surname (which has an alternative form, Millar) and as a profession. It was first used in English in the fourteenth century, even though the miller has played an important role in all societies since the Stone Age.

In its most primitive form the act of milling was quite simple. The wheat or corn was harvested from a field and then placed between two large circular stones, the top one of which was turned so as to grind the grain and release the flour within. This was then collected and could be made into bread, the staple diet of most European peoples. But this is something of an oversimplification; using the

Words for 'miller' in different European languages are strikingly similar. Notice how the following begin with virtually the same letters, although slightly modified in some cases.

Bulgarian	*melnichar*
Danish	*miller*
Dutch	*molenaar*
Estonian	*mölder*
German	*Müller*
Hungarian	*molnár*
Icelandic	*miller*
Irish	*muilneoir*
Russian	*mel'nik*
Spanish	*molinero*
Italian	*molinaro*
Greek	*milonás*
Welsh	*melinydd*

quern (from the Old English *cweorn*, 'hand mill') was hard, physically demanding work, which is why we still talk about 'the daily grind'. And there are other metaphorical expressions we have derived from the millers of the past: 'it's all grist to the mill', 'a millstone around our necks' and 'to put someone through the mill'.

The Old English for 'to mill' was *mylen*, a verb based on the Latin words *mola*, 'grindstone', and *molere*, 'to grind', which etymologists trace back to the Indo-European root **mele*, meaning 'to crush'. And such a provenance has meant that we now have many words in English which are cognate with the descendants of the same root: 'molar', a tooth designed for grinding food; 'meal', grain that has been ground; 'emolument', now synonymous with 'payment', but originally money paid by a farmer to a miller for grinding his corn. Perhaps the most surprising, however, is 'maelstrom', which we tend to think of as a whirlpool, but is literally a 'pool that grinds'.

Minister

If a person is described quite simply as being a 'minister', such is the wide variety of meanings the word can have that additional information is almost always required. The man or woman concerned might be a minister of religion (usually Nonconformist or Presbyterian, and almost always Protestant), or he or she could hold high office in government, perhaps as the minister of state for defence or education. Whatever the case, the term is always applied to people acting for, or under the authority of, somebody else.

The word was first used in an ecclesiastical context circa 1300 and represented something of a degree of social promotion. Prior to its application to members of the church it had been used in Old French as *ministre*, meaning 'servant' or 'member of the household staff'. And the status of anyone so described would have been very low, as can be seen in the word's derivation: it is ultimately derived from the Latin *minister*, an 'inferior', related to the words *minus*, 'less', and *minor*, 'smaller'. But the noun *minister* was also used in Latin to designate a priest's 'assistant', a usage which possibly contributed to the eventual rise up the social ladder. In a non-ecclesiastical setting, the social elevation of the word reached its climax in the 1620s when it was first used to designate high office of state.

During the thirteenth century, another closely related word had also appeared. The Old French word *ministre* had changed into *menestrel*, defining a servant with particular talents, namely a facility for storytelling, composing poetry and entertaining the lords and ladies with his singing and musical virtuosity. This talented young man became the English 'minstrel', who features so prominently in the history of the Middle Ages.

> The Minstrel-Boy to the war is gone,
>> In the ranks of death you'll find him;
> His father's sword he has girded on,
>> And his wild harp slung behind him.
>>>> THOMAS MOORE, 'The Minstrel-Boy' (1807)

Nurse

A professional nurse is somebody who, after a lengthy period of training and years of study, is qualified to look after the sick in a hospital or similar institution. And under the banner of 'nursing' there is a whole host of specialisms and specialist nurses: psychiatric, midwifery, cardiac, perioperative and so on. But the idea of a 'nurse' tending people who are ill or in need of medical attention dates from no earlier than the 1580s, and the verb 'to nurse' was not recorded before 1736. In the Middle Ages a nurse would more normally be found *in loco parentis*, bringing up children of the nobility, washing, feeding and dressing them as well as possibly introducing them to the basics of education.

The word entered English in the twelfth century as *nurrice*, primarily meaning a 'wet nurse', but the term was also applied to a foster-mother to a child or children who, for one reason or another, could not be cared for by their parents. (From the Old English *fōstrian*, 'to feed', 'to nourish'. Also related is the Old Norse *fóstra*, 'nurse'.) The Old French term from which *nurrice* was taken was *norrice*, one of the sources of the name Norris, first recorded as a surname in England in the twelfth century.

Ultimately, however, the word 'nurse' is derived from the Latin *nutrix*, who in Ancient Rome could also be a foster-mother or a wet nurse. But the associated verb here, *nutrire*, is a good indication of the concept behind the noun; its primary meaning was 'to suckle'. Therefore, etymologically speaking, the original meaning of 'nurse' was 'one who suckles', which makes the modern term 'male nurse' somewhat problematic from a linguist's point of view.

Quite a few other words we use in English are directly related etymologically to 'nurse', including 'nutrition', 'nursery' (for children and plants), 'nurture', 'nutrient', 'nutritious'. The common denominator here is that they are all associated with feeding, rearing and offering succour.

> O sleep, O gentle sleep,
> Nature's soft nurse, how have I frighted thee,
> That thou no more wilt weigh my eyelids down
> And steep my senses in forgetfulness?
>
> WILLIAM SHAKESPEARE, *2 Henry IV* (1597?), 3.1

Optician

Since the sixteenth century, many words in English associated with the eyes have begun with the letters 'op-'. The study of sight is 'optics'; if we need to have our eyes examined we go to the 'optician'; if we then need spectacles an 'optometrist' will do the measuring involved and provide them for us.

The Greek word at the base of all these words is *optikós*, 'visible', an adjective derived from the noun *ōps*, meaning 'eye'. But the same Greek noun also shows up in other words commonly found in modern English. An 'autopsy', for instance, is an examination of a dead body which allows the pathologist to assess the cause of death. Literally, it is a process which allows the medical specialist to 'see for himself' (Greek *autos*, 'self', plus *ōps*) why a person died. Still in the world of medicine, a 'biopsy' allows another specialist to 'see living organisms' (Greek *bios*, 'life', plus *ōps*). And, more generally, a 'synopsis' is a brief summation of a long document or book. This is again Greek, comprising *syn*, 'together', 'all at once', and *ōps*, suggesting that a 'synopsis' brings all the main points of a document together at the same time.

The Greeks also had another word for the eye: *ophthalmos*, which forms the basis of the modern medical term 'ophthalmologist', a medically qualified specialist who treats diseases of the eye. It is now generally agreed among etymologists that this is a combination of *ōps* and *thalamos*, 'chamber'. And the 'chamber' in this case is the 'eye socket', reminding us that the ophthalmologist's preoccupation is not just with the eye but with its surrounding area as well.

> Drink to me only with thine eyes
> And I will pledge with mine;
> Or leave a kiss but in the cup,
> And I'll not look for wine.

BEN JONSON, 'To Celia' (1616)

Pardoner

Perhaps not all but arguably some pardoners were the medieval versions of today's 'con artists'. They were officially licensed to sell papal pardons and indulgences; but, as there were few (if any) checks and balances on their activities, the temptation to divert church funds for their own benefit frequently proved too great.

Geoffrey Chaucer (*c.* 1343–1400) includes a pardoner in his *Canterbury Tales* and so highlights the devious ploys these churchmen employed in order to dupe ordinary members of the public into donating money, nominally to the church, but more often than not into their own purses. Chaucer's pardoner carried a bag of pigs' bones, claiming that they were the relics of saints and that anyone who touched them, for a fee, would have their sins absolved. And the poet, taking a swipe at the church, has the pardoner admit that he did not care a fig for the souls of those he was claiming to save from damnation. The only thing he cared about was separating the 'sinners' from their cash and so would use all manner of psychological scams, preying on his victims' gullibility, to end the day with a bulging purse.

The derivation of the word 'pardoner' is the old French *pardun*, 'pardon', from the Medieval Latin *perdonare*, 'to concede', 'to remit punishment for sins committed'. The root of the verb was *donare*, 'to give', and the prefix *per*, originally 'through' but eventually also 'thorough', so that *perdonare* came to mean 'to give thorough' absolution, thereby guaranteeing a smooth passage to Heaven.

From a linguistic point of view there is an interesting comparison to be made here. One meaning of the Latin *per* is 'for', and the English for *donare* is 'to give'; by combining the two we get 'forgive', which has exactly the same meaning as the Latin.

By the 1540s the idea of 'pardoning' someone had lost many of its ecclesiastical associations and was being used generally to excuse very minor faults or insignificant errors.

||||||||||||||||||||||||||||||||||||||||||||||||||||||||||||||||||||||||||||||||||||||||||||||||||||||||||

Other medieval occupations mentioned in
The Canterbury Tales:

FRIAR A priest with no allegiance to any particular monastery, he would normally live and work in the community. Name derived from the French *frère*, 'brother'.

SUMMONER Employed to conduct those accused of breaking church law to an ecclesiastic court.

MANCIPLE Employed by a college or court to make sure there was a constant supply of food and wine. Derived from the Latin *manus*, 'hand', and *capere*, 'to seize', 'to obtain'.

FRANKLIN Literally 'free man'. A landowner of free but not noble birth.

REEVE Local law officer. In Anglo-Saxon times a man of considerable authority at a local level.

YEOMAN In the fourteenth century, an attendant below the rank of sergeant. Etymologists dispute the origin of the word, but it is possibly just a contraction of 'young man'.

||||||||||||||||||||||||||||||||||||||||||||||||||||||||||||||||||||||||||||||||||||||||||||||||||||||||||

Photographer

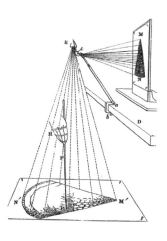

The person we have to thank for the terms 'photographer' and 'photography' is Sir John Herschel (1792–1871), a Victorian chemist, mathematician and all-round polymath, who was fascinated by what others had done in the early stages of what came to be known as photography. Cameras of varying degrees of sophistication had been known for centuries; the Ancient Greeks, Chinese and Arabs (among others) were aware of the 'pin-hole' camera effect, and Leonardo da Vinci (1452–1519) observed that an upside-down image could be projected onto a piece of paper by light from the sun shining through a chink in a cave wall. The problem, however, was one of retaining the projected image so that it survived on the paper after the source of the light had disappeared. And this is where the early-nineteenth-century 'photographers' came into their own.

On 14 March 1839 Herschel delivered a paper to an august gathering of the Royal Society, during which he used the term 'photography' for the first time. Honouring the custom of the day among the scientific community, he borrowed Greek roots to define the newly emerging

131

science. As he and his associates in the field were essentially finding ways of etching light-generated images onto a suitable surface, he used the Greek *phōs* (genitive *phōtos*), meaning 'light', combined it with the verb *graphein*, 'to write' (but originally 'to scratch'), and thus coined 'photography', 'photographer' and 'photographic'. The related 'photogenic', suggesting that someone or something would make a good subject for a photograph, was first recorded in 1928.

It was also Herschel who discovered a method of photo-printing images onto suitably sensitized surfaces. As anything printed by this method had a bluish tint, his term for the process was (resorting to Greek once again) 'cyanotype', based on the Greek *kuanos*, 'blue', and *tupos*, 'impression', 'image', giving us another word now used in a wide variety of contexts: 'blueprint'.

> My aspirations are to ennoble Photography and to secure
> for it the character and uses of High Art by combining
> the real & Ideal & sacrificing nothing of Truth by all
> possible devotion to poetry and beauty.
>
> JULIA MARGARET CAMERON
> to Sir John Herschel, 31 December 1864

Pilot

We now understand a pilot to be the man or woman whose role it is to fly our aeroplane and make sure we arrive safely. When the word was adopted into English in the early sixteenth century, however, it referred to a helmsman steering a ship through choppy waters and bringing it to a safe haven.

The reason the same word can be applied to a plane or a boat is quite simple. When men developed the technology that allowed them to leave dry land for the second time and fly through the air, they retained much of the terminology they used the first time, when they put to sea. We still talk about 'boarding' a plane; the personnel are referred to as the 'cabin crew'; and the left- and right-hand sides of an aircraft are always referred to as 'port' and 'starboard'. When the first balloons took to the skies in the eighteenth century, the daring young men operating the contraptions were called 'aeronauts' (hence 'aeronautics', the science of flight), a word invented by combining the Greek for 'air', *aēr*, and *nautēs*, 'sailor'. Later, in the twentieth century, the Zeppelin and the *Hindenburg*, hailed

at the time as the transport of the future, were enormous 'air-ships', beneath which the crew travelled in a 'gondola', originally a vessel only found on the canals of Venice.

'Pilot' was borrowed from the French *pilote*, derived probably from the fourteenth-century Italian word *piloto*, an adaptation of *pedotta*, which is thought to have been based on a cluster of Greek words: *pēdon*, 'oar'; *pēdalion*, 'rudder'; and *pēdotēs*, which in Medieval Greek meant both 'rudder' and 'helmsman'. And all these Greek words are related to another Greek noun, *pous* (genitive *podos*), meaning 'foot', the most primitive of all guidance systems.

Many words in English are cognate with the Greek for 'foot', but perhaps the most significant one in this context is 'pedal', as, when we get down to basics, the pilot of an aircraft has, since 1907, been the person with their 'foot' on the 'pedal'.

Plastic surgeon

Plastic surgery is not new. The vast array of high-tech, complicated technology at the disposal of modern exponents of the art gives the impression that the world in which plastic surgeons work is a twenty-first-century phenomenon, but this is not the case. In ancient times, forerunners of our modern doctors attempted to reshape and repair damaged limbs and flesh when our ancestors had been involved in terrible accidents or had returned disfigured from a war. We have evidence that in Ancient Greece, Rome and Egypt, facial reconstruction was attempted, and in Haridwar (India) there is a statue to a certain Shushruta, who in the sixth century BCE left written accounts of how reconstructive surgery should be approached.

The first use of the term 'plastic' in a surgical context was in 1839, although the word had been used in English since the mid-seventeenth century, borrowed from the French *plastique* and the Latin *plasticus*, meaning 'can be shaped'. And both of these were closely related to the Greek *plastikē tekhnē*, which simply meant 'the art of moulding', based on the verb *plassein*, 'to mould', 'to shape'.

'Plastic surgeons' rearrange patients' features for purely medical considerations; a 'cosmetic surgeon', on the other hand, performs more or less the same operations simply because the customer wishes to alter his or her appearance for personal reasons. And 'cosmetic' is another word of Greek derivation; *kosmos* meant 'order' (things 'in order' to the Greeks were automatically 'beautiful'), suggesting that if 'plastic surgeons' perform 'cosmetic surgery' they are 'shaping' parts of a person's body with the aim of altering the 'order' in which Nature intended them to be.

And the word 'surgeon'? This is simply a corrupted form of two Greek words, *kheir*, 'hand', and *ergon*, 'work', which when combined mean nothing more than 'someone who works with his hands'.

Plumber

When the word 'plumber' was first used in English in the late fourteenth century it was not associated with the installation of pipes, baths and shower systems in people's homes, as it is today. In medieval English society the term was reserved for just about any workman or tradesman who used lead in their job, particularly roofers, who found the metal extremely easy to work with. It was relatively soft and could be melted down and then easily moulded to almost any shape required. In fact, it could hardly be bettered as a material for waterproofing a building.

The word acquired its more specific meaning in the nineteenth century when it became increasingly more common to construct houses with their own, individually controllable, water supply. People no longer had to rely on a nearby stream or well for their water; the age had dawned when they could just turn on a tap and the water would flow. And the person whom they had to thank for installing the marvellous social innovation was the local 'plumber', who, despite the fact that most, if not all, water pipes now are made of copper, still enjoys the title today.

The precursor to the word in English was the Old French *plumier*, the trade description of any man who worked with lead for a living. The derivation of this word was the Latin *plumbarius*, an adjective meaning 'relating to lead', but eventually used as a noun to define the Roman worker who lined water channels with lead or sealed roofs with it to keep the rain out. And the terminus of this etymological road was the Latin noun *plumbum*, 'lead', distantly related to the Greek *molubdos*, also meaning 'lead', and the basis of the metallic element we know as 'molybdenum'.

Nobody has been able to ascertain with any confidence the origin of the word 'lead'. It has been suggested that it could be Celtic in origin, a theory supported by the fact that the modern Irish is *luaidhe*. This is known to be related to the German *Lot*, a cognate of 'lead' and meaning what we normally refer to as a 'plummet' or 'plumb line'.

> Fly, envious Time, till thou run out thy race,
> Call on the lazy, leaden-stepping hours,
> Whose speed is but the heavy Plummets pace
>
> JOHN MILTON, 'On Time' (1645)

Policeman/policewoman

Policemen and policewomen are servants of the law whose main duty is to protect other members of society from those who might wish to do them harm. But before the eighteenth century, public order was something of a hit-and-miss affair, largely dependent on the medieval concept of 'hue and cry', whereby individual members of the community were required to respond to any calls to pursue and apprehend a miscreant.

Henry Fielding, magistrate and novelist, lived at 4 Bow Street, London; in 1789 he set up the Bow Street Runners, who are traditionally considered to be the embryonic civil protection organization we recognize today as the police. Then, in about 1798, the Marine Police were established in London to prevent the theft of goods passing through the port. Some years later, in 1829, the Home Secretary, Sir Robert Peel, created the Metropolitan Police to deal with the ever-growing crime rate in the capital. The etymology of the word is a constant reminder that the first 'policemen' pounded the beat on the streets of a large 'city'.

The word 'police', as applied to a civil organization charged with defending the general public, was borrowed in the late fifteenth century from the French *police*, and the Medieval Latin *politia*, simply meaning 'civil administration'. This in turn was a direct borrowing of the Ancient Greek *polis*, an independent 'city state' such as Athens or Sparta.

When we talk today about 'the police' we invariably use the word as a noun, but strictly speaking it is the adjective in a phrase such as 'the police force', meaning 'the force guarding the *polis* or city'.

Other words found in English containing the word *polis* include: metropolis ('mother city'), cosmopolitan ('citizen of the world'), necropolis ('city of the dead' – i.e. cemetery). And then there are place names such as: the Acropolis ('the city at the top'), Naples (in Italian *Napoli*, from the Greek *nea polis*, 'new city') and, in Libya, Tripoli ('three cities', as it was originally three North African cities, which merged into one).

Postman/postwoman

In a sense, the idea of a 'postman' or 'postwoman' walking around town delivering letters and small parcels to offices and private houses contradicts the derivation of the word; 'post' is synonymous with 'position' and is therefore more suggestive of a static state than of motion. Etymologically the word 'post' is linked to the Italian *posto*, 'place', and the Latin *positum*, the past participle of the infinitive *ponere*, 'to put', so that a 'post' was originally a place where someone or something 'had been put'.

Henry VIII (r. 1509–47) realized that a functioning postal system was essential if important letters and documents were to be dispatched to all corners of his realm and expected to arrive safely. He therefore appointed, in 1516, the first Master of the Posts (the job title was changed to Postmaster General in 1710), who oversaw a relay delivery system not dissimilar to America's 'Pony Express' a couple of centuries later.

In July 1635 Charles I (r. 1625–49) decreed that the system of delivering letters countrywide be made available to the general public with post offices dotted up and down the country, effectively creating the Royal Mail. In those

days, however, it was the recipient of a letter or package who paid, not the sender.

In Britain we now have both the Post Office and the Royal Mail, and postmen can deliver either 'the post' or 'the mail', as the terms are virtually inter-changeable. Etymologically, however, there is a difference.

'Post' referred originally to letters and parcels conveyed by men 'posted' at intervals along the road network; 'mail' did not refer to the letters but to the bag in which they were carried. In Middle English *male* meant 'bag' and was a borrowing from the Old French *male*, with the same meaning, although this is thought to be from a Germanic root. And *male* (Middle English and Old French) has a linguistic relative in Irish Gaelic, which still has *mala* as the normal word for 'bag'.

For evil news rides post, while good news baits.*

JOHN MILTON, Samson Agonistes (1671)

* 'Baits' here means to break off a journey for food and rest at an inn.

Priest

Generally speaking, a priest is an ordained minister of religion who officiates at religious ceremonies and, in some religions, is believed to intercede between men and God, a god or gods.

In Anglo-Saxon England the man who officiated at religious ceremonies was the *prēost*, a term of Germanic origin, compressed and borrowed from the Late Latin *presbyter*. But the Late Latin word was itself a borrowing from the Greek *presbuteros*, meaning 'elder' (technically, it is the comparative of the adjective *presbus*, 'old'), in much the same way that the word 'senior' is derived from the Latin noun *senex*, 'old man'. Taken together, the Greek and Latin terms suggest that, for the ancients, old age was a qualification for positions of authority.

But there is another theory. Some etymologists have suggested that the word 'priest' is actually cognate with the Old High German *priast*, derived from the Vulgar Latin *prevost*. This is a contraction of the Latin *praepositus*, comprising *prae*, 'in front', and *positus*, 'placed', and so means 'person placed at the front', implying that such an individual would stand in front of, and lead, the congregation.

In the sixteenth century the Greek word *presbuteros* was borrowed again in its full form by Calvin and his followers in Scotland, who wished to break away from the dominance of the Church of England with its clerical hierarchy headed by an archbishop and his bishops. They preferred their organization to be governed and administered by a council of 'elders' and so took to calling themselves 'Presbyterians'.

Anglers, of course, have another interpretation of the word 'priest'. When a fisherman pulls a fish out of the water he will usually put it out of its misery by hitting it on the head with a specially designed little hammer. This is also known as a 'priest', because it is the instrument by which the last rights are administered to the fish.

> By education most have been misled;
> So they believe, because they were so bred.
> The priest continues what the nurse began,
> And thus the child imposes on the man.
>
> JOHN DRYDEN, *The Hind and the Panther* (1687)

Publican

Few would now think of a publican as anything other than a keeper of a public house. But this has not always been the case. The first known example of an 'inn keeper' being referred to as a publican was in the first half of the eighteenth century. Prior to this date and as far back as *c.* 1200 a publican was not the cheery 'mine host', but the less than socially popular tax gatherer. To understand this transformation, we have to go back to Ancient Rome and trace the evolution of the term from there.

The Roman tax collector was known as a *publicanus*, an adjective used as a noun and derived from the word *publicum*, 'public revenue', 'treasury'. And the root of these words was another noun, *populus*, 'people', and its related adjective *publicus*, 'belonging to the people'.

Early in the fifteenth century the derivative word 'public', meaning 'pertaining to the people', made its way into English and found uses in several contexts. One of these was in the expression 'public house', denoting an establishment where entertainment of various sorts was made available to the 'public'. At this time a place designed specifically for the selling and consumption of ales and wine was usually referred to as 'an inn'; the first reference to a 'pub' dates from 1768, although the landlord of such a hostelry was first recorded as a 'publican' some years earlier in 1728.

The older, more traditional 'inn' dates back to Anglo-Saxon times, when an *inn* was simply a dwelling place or somewhere a weary traveller could find a night's lodgings. In the Middle Ages it acquired the more specific designation of what we would probably refer to as a 'students' accommodation block'. And this explains why, even in the twenty-first century, we still refer to the 'inns of court' and can boast such institutions as 'Gray's Inn' and 'Lincoln's Inn'.

And it will no doubt come as no surprise that the word *inn* basically just means 'in'; it derives from the Old English *innan*, meaning 'in', 'inside'. The original meaning, therefore, was almost certainly simply a building where, on a freezing winter's night, our forebears could get 'inside' and thaw out.

> Like pilgrims to th'appointed place we tend;
> The world's an inn, and death the journey's end.
>
> JOHN DRYDEN, *Palamon and Arcite* (1700)

Pundit

On 31 December 1600 Queen Elizabeth I of England granted a royal charter to a company of London traders, which then became known as the East India Company. Its role was to engage in trade with the newly discovered East Indies (formerly East India), and thus began an association between Britain and India which was to endure until 1947.

Originally a commercial organization, the East India Company soon found itself ruling (it even had its own private army) and administering what was to become known as British India, an arrangement that lasted until 1858 when the British government assumed all responsibility for the governance of the subcontinent. Such intimate contact with the vast country, with twenty-two major languages and thirteen different scripts, meant that inevitably words of Indian origin soon began to percolate into English. One such word was 'pundit'.

It is first recorded in English in the 1670s when it retained the original Sanskrit meaning of a priest or Brahman who had studied, and was well versed in, ancient Sanskrit lore. But in Hindi, the related language with which the British would have had more contact, *payndit* (or *paṇḍit*) had become a common term for 'master' or 'teacher'.

By the nineteenth century 'pundit' (alternatively 'pandit') was widely used in English and had acquired the meaning we attach to it today: an expert in a given field who is frequently invited to comment on an issue or event in public.

IIIIIIIIIIIIIIIIIIIIIIIIIIIIIIIIIIIIIIIIIIIIIIIIIIIIIIIIIIIIIIIIIIIIIIIIIIIIIIIIIIIIIIIIIIIIIIIIIIIIIIIIIII

Some other words in English derived from Hindi:

Bungalow	A house built by Europeans in Bengal.
Chutney	From the infinitive *caṭnī*, 'to lick'.
Khaki	From *khaki*, meaning 'dusty', 'dust coloured'.
Punch	The drink known as punch takes its name from the word *pañca*, meaning 'five', a reference to its five ingredients.
Shampoo	From *câpo*, an imperative meaning 'rub!'
Tickety-boo	From *thik hai, babu*, 'That's OK, master.'
Cushy	From *kuš*, 'excellent', 'healthy', 'happy'.

IIIIIIIIIIIIIIIIIIIIIIIIIIIIIIIIIIIIIIIIIIIIIIIIIIIIIIIIIIIIIIIIIIIIIIIIIIIIIIIIIIIIIIIIIIIIIIIIIIIIIIIIIII

Restaurateur

In 1796 the English borrowed the French word *restaurateur* as a term to define the proprietor of a 'restaurant'. But the word 'restaurant' originally was an adjective applied to what was on sale in the establishment, not the hostelry itself.

Some years earlier, in 1765, a citizen of Paris hit on the idea of offering for sale *bouillons restaurants*, literally 'restorative broths', intended to satisfy people's hunger and 'restore' their sagging energy levels and enthusiasm for getting on with the chores of the day.

The first of these 'restaurants' was opened very close to the Louvre. The proprietor had another brainwave when wondering how he could entice the hungry populace through his door. He borrowed a Latin phrase, very loosely based on a verse from the New Testament (Matthew 11:28), which he hung in the window: *venite ad me omnes qui stomacho laboratis et ego vos restaurabo* ('come to me all whose stomachs are afflicted and I will restore you'). Presumably his tactic worked, as 'restaurants' and 'restaurateurs' have been with us ever since.

And the name of this enterprising Parisian? Nobody has been able to establish his first name, as all the extant documents simply refer to him as 'Monsieur Boulanger', which, rather appropriately for someone in the hospitality business, translates into English as 'Mr Baker'.

Scavenger

The word 'scavenger' now applies universally to a person who roots about for what they can find in the rubbish discarded by others. Or it can apply to animals that roam the streets or countryside looking for scraps to eat. But the original scavengers enjoyed a far more elevated position in society: they were in fact town officials whose job it was to make sure that markets were swept and tidied up after close of business.

In the sixteenth century a 'scavager' (the original form of the word) was charged with patrolling the markets of London, making sure that any traders from outside the town had paid 'scavage', a toll paid in exchange for permission to display goods for sale. And the word 'display' is a clue to the derivation of the word; it derives from the Flemish *scauwen*, 'to show', as the first 'scavengers' simply made sure that stallholders had paid for the right to 'show' what they had for sale.

The market official's preoccupation with detritus and rubbish explains our interpretation of the word 'scavenger' today.

Scribe

Most people will recognize this word, even if it does not feature in their everyday vocabulary. And they will make frequent use of many words derived from it, such as 'describe', 'inscribe', 'prescribe', 'scripture' and many more.

Historically, a scribe was a professional writer who, in the days when few people could write, kept records, wrote correspondence and performed many of the duties we would today associate with secretarial tasks. His role (and it was usually a man until relatively recently) was socially very important; it is due to the written records so meticulously kept by these professional 'scribblers' that modern historians are able to learn so much about the cultures and lifestyles of societies that flourished and faded centuries, if not millennia, ago.

The derivation of the word 'scribe', and all those associated with it, is the Latin verb *scribere*, 'to write', which itself can be traced back to the Indo-European root *skribh*, meaning 'to scratch'. The connection is obvious; the earliest forms of writing were little more than scratchings on stone or clay.

There is a commonly used expression which is frequently heard in English and is directly connected with this word, even if we do not recognize it as such. If we dismiss someone contemptuously and without giving due consideration to what they have to say, we are said to 'give them short shrift'. And a 'shrift' (also derived from *scribere*) from the 1590s onwards was a written penance demanded (or perhaps recommended) by the church before a guilty man or woman was executed. The original 'short shrift' relates to the brief time a miscreant was given to write down his or her sins between sentence being passed and execution being carried out.

Also related is the period on the Christian calendar known as Shrovetide. Since the fifteenth century this has referred to the three days before Lent (from the Old English *lencten*, meaning spring) when Christians were expected to make full confession of their sins, originally in written form.

> Come, come: dispatch: the duke would be at dinner.
> Make a short shrift; he longs to see your head.
>
> WILLIAM SHAKESPEARE, *Richard III* (1594), 3.4

Scullery maid

Aficionados of the television historical dramas set in the grand houses of the nobility will be well acquainted with the scullery maid. She is the timid little girl at the very bottom of the domestic hierarchy; the 'drudge' who has to be at everybody else's beck and call, night and day, tidying up and making sure the kitchen is clean and tidy.

The job of a scullery maid (her male equivalent was an etymologically unrelated 'scullion') was arduous and physically demanding. She not only had to clean the pots and pans, but also had to scrub the floor, clean the grate, the stoves, the sinks and, when she had done all that, wash the dishes. But she was not to be trusted with the crystal, silver or china; such articles were far too delicate and valuable to be entrusted to a mere slip of a girl. Only the housemaids and footmen, who occupied a more elevated position in the household, could be trusted to clean them without damaging or breaking them.

The scullery maid's domain was the scullery. This was a smaller room situated just off the main kitchen and nearest the best source of water, as vast amounts were needed for her to complete all her duties satisfactorily. The word was first used in English in the mid-fifteenth century and referred to the part of the house intended for the storing and maintenance of dishes. It is derived from the Old French *escuelerie*, derived in turn from another word, *escuele*, meaning 'dish'. And both of these words trace their origins back to the Latin words *scutella*, a 'flat dish', and *scutra*, which was a cruder platter fashioned out of a plank of wood.

> Away, you scullion, you rampallian, you fustilarian! I'll tickle your catastrophe!
>
> WILLIAM SHAKESPEARE, *2 King Henry IV* (1596–99), 2.1

Secretary

Secretaries are often jokingly referred to as 'goalkeepers' because they stand between their bosses and other employees, making sure that access to the boss's office is strictly by appointment. They are also largely responsible for the smooth running of the office, as they organize the boss's diary, arrange meetings, keep the minutes and put their keyboard skills and competence with a computer to good use.

In the fourteenth century a 'secretary' was a confidant (literally, someone who 'can be trusted'), as such a person would be more likely to keep one's 'secrets' secret. By the fifteenth century the meaning had widened somewhat to include employees who were paid to keep records and take charge of any correspondence. A century later the term was being applied to senior civil servants who ran government departments, and survives today in titles such as Home Secretary, Secretary of State and so on.

The word itself entered Middle English as a derivative (via Old French) of the Latin *secretus*, 'separate', an adjective derived from the verb *secernere*, 'to set aside', a compound of *se*, 'apart', and *cernere*, 'to sift'. By Late Latin times the noun *secretarius* had evolved and acquired the meaning of 'confidential officer', whose job, etymologically speaking, was to 'sift' information not meant for public consumption and keep it 'secret' or 'apart' from what could be safely made known to a wider audience.

Of course, a secretary needs somewhere to work and possibly store away documents in a relatively secure place. In eighteenth-century France such requirements produced the *secrétaire*, a special desk with a writing surface as well as drawers and possibly hidden compartments where documents could be 'secreted' away from prying eyes. By the nineteenth century the word had been adopted into English as 'secretaire'.

A curious connection here is the African, snake-eating 'secretary bird'. It takes its name from its distinctive head plumage, with swept-back feathers which reminded nineteenth-century explorers of many secretaries' habit of tucking quills behind their ears.

> I know that's a secret, for it's whispered everywhere.
> WILLIAM CONGREVE, *Love for Love* (1695)

Sheriff

For many of us the sheriff is the man who, in Hollywood westerns, wears a tin star and packs a six-gun. Or (and again we have Hollywood to thank here) the word conjures up images of the nefarious Sheriff of Nottingham in films about the quasi-mythical outlaw in feudal England, Robin Hood. The term is still used (frequently in less dramatic contexts) throughout the world to define officers involved in upholding or enforcing the law.

The word originated in Anglo-Saxon England where the *scīrgerēfa* (the Old English form of 'sheriff') was a figure of authority with a variety of administrative and legal duties to fulfil. His role as the person responsible for the maintenance of law and order can still be seen in Scotland where the term is applied to the judge in a court of law.

The Old English *scīrgerēfa* was a combination of two words: *scīr*, which had several meanings, one of which was what came to be known as a 'county' but which prior to the Norman conquest was a 'shire'. The second element of the word, *gerēfa* (derived from *rēfa*, more recognizable in its modern form, 'reeve'), originally referred to the man charged with looking after a landowner's estate, but who gradually shouldered other responsibilities in his capacity as a guardian of the peace.

When the Normans arrived in England in 1066 they imposed many of their laws and much of their legal terminology on the native population. Whereas the Anglo-Saxons had divided their country into 'shires', their Norman masters insisted that the country divisions be called 'counties', and that each one should be administered by a 'count'. Consequently, the situation in modern Britain is that we now speak of both 'shires' and 'counties', if sometimes inconsistently: we have, for example, Lanca*shire* and York*shire* but '*county* Durham' and 'the *county* of Kent'.

In Britain, we have never used the title 'count', but have always preferred to appoint a duke as the monarch's representative of a county.

> In Summertime on Bredon
> The bells they sound so clear;
> Round both the shires they ring them
> In steeples far and near,
> A happy noise to hear.

A.E. HOUSMAN, 'Bredon Hill' (1896)

Shipwreck hunter

Today it is estimated that, worldwide, something in the region of 3 million sunken ships lie on the seabed, some of them still containing artefacts and treasure which, once salvaged, could fetch enormous sums on the open market. And the people who chase these submerged riches are known as 'shipwreck hunters', which strictly speaking is incorrect.

The noun 'wreck' has existed in English since the thirteenth century (originally an Anglo-Norman legal term) and is a derivative of the Old Norse verb *reka*, 'to drive', 'to thrust', so that 'a wreck' or 'wreckage' refers, from a purely etymological point of view, to the remains of a ship that have been 'thrust' ashore by the waves, not to what lies at the bottom of the sea.

There is an additional etymological connection here which few people would suspect. Shipwrecks gave us the word 'average'. The fifteenth-century form of the word was *averys* (based on the French and Italian forms, *avarie* and *avaria* respectively), meaning a charge levied for the shipment of freight. But part of the charge covered the possibility of the cargo being lost or damaged in transit, and by the sixteenth century the sense of the word had shifted to mean not only cargo lost at sea, but also the equitable distribution of the losses among those who had paid the shipping costs. By the eighteenth century the term 'average' was applied more generally to define an arithmetical mean in any context, just as it is today.

The Arabic word *awāriya*, 'damage to goods', was the original term from which the other concepts were borrowed and later developed.

> Antonio hath a ship of rich lading wrecked on the narrow seas – the Goodwins I think they call the place – a very dangerous flat, and fatal, where the carcasses of many a tall ship lie buried.
>
> WILLIAM SHAKESPEARE, *The Merchant of Venice* (1596–99?), 3.1

Sky marshal

Most of us are probably unaware, as we fly around the globe, that we are being guarded by plain-clothes protection agents blending in with the other passengers but ready to spring into action in the event of a terrorist attempting to hijack (or skyjack) the plane. These derring-do men or women of action have been referred to as 'sky marshals' since the 1960s.

The term 'sky marshal' is a relatively new coining, based on two ancient words. In Anglo-Saxon England the word 'sky' referred to what we now call a 'cloud'; it did not acquire its present-day meaning until the thirteenth century. In Old English it was a *scēo*, related to the Old Norse *sky*, from the Indo-European root *(s)keu*, 'to cover', 'to obscure'. And what we see when we look upwards and call the 'sky' was, for the Anglo-Saxons, *heofon*, or, as we now say, 'heaven'.

Interestingly, in Middle English 'sky' could be used for both 'cloud' and 'heaven', and therefore had a plural form when referring to a number of clouds. This explains why we can, in modern English, praise somebody 'to the skies'.

When 'marshal' entered English in the thirteenth century it was a title applied to a high-ranking officer at a royal court whose main responsibility was the organization of official ceremonies. Prior to this he had been known in France as a *mareschal*, a commanding officer in an army. And *mareschal* had worked its way into French from the Old High German *marahscalh*, the root of which was *mare*, 'horse' (our word 'mare'), which denoted the 'servant who looked after the horses'. In other words, the terms 'marshal', 'henchman' and 'constable' are essentially the same in meaning.

> And that inverted Bowl we call The Sky,
> Whereunder crawling coop'd we live and die,
> Lift not thy hands to *It* for help – for It
> Rolls impotently on as Thou or I.
> EDWARD FITZGERALD, The Rubaiyat of Omar Khayyam
(1859)

Smith

The image of the burly blacksmith bringing down his hammer onto an anvil is not an entirely accurate reflection of the original meaning of this word; historically a 'smith' was any skilled worker. In fact, in Anglo-Saxon England the word 'smith' was also applied to people we now think of exclusively as carpenters.

For an explanation of this apparent confusion we have to travel back in time to when our Indo-European ancestors were wandering around the Great European

Plain. The original Indo-European language contained a root *smi-, which is found at the base of many words in modern European languages in connection with the idea of 'cutting' or 'working with a sharp instrument'. Ancient Greek, for instance, had the words *smilē* and *smileuma*, meaning 'carving knife' and 'carvings' respectively.

In the fifteenth century the word 'blacksmith' entered English and was applied specifically to the man who toiled away all day, moving between furnace and anvil, as he fashioned items vital to the community such as gates, tools, horseshoes and all manner of agricultural implements. He took his name from the 'black metal' (i.e. iron) with which he worked.

But 'black' was not the only colour to combine with the word 'smith' in the Middle Ages. There were also 'whitesmiths' (who worked with tin or pewter), brownsmiths (copper or brass) and 'redsmiths', who confined themselves to producing goods made out of copper. 'Goldsmiths' and 'silversmiths' take their names from the metals with which they work, although coincidentally these are colours also.

Interestingly, the original meaning of a smith as any sort of skilled operative has re-emerged in more modern trade definitions, such as 'wordsmith', 'gunsmith', 'locksmith' etc. And perhaps we should also mention the modern slang 'fingersmith', which can be applied to both a pickpocket and a midwife!

'Smith', first recorded as a surname in England in the tenth century, is today the commonest surname of all. It also features as a trade and family name in many other cultures, including:

German	Schmidt
Polish	Kowalski
Hungarian	Kovacs
Russian	Kuznetsov
French	Lefèvre
Spanish	Herrara
Arabic	Haddad
Danish	Smed
Irish	MacGowan

Soldier

In Anglo-Saxon England the word for 'war' was *wīg* and the man who went off to fight the foe and defend his plot of land was a *wiga* or a *wīgbora*. Around the year 1300 the word was superseded by the Old French *soudier* or *soldier*, both of which were derivatives of the noun *soulde*, meaning 'a soldier's pay'. In other words, a 'soldier' was originally a man who went off to fight in exchange for payment.

Soulde was a corruption of the Latin *solidus* (also the origin of our word 'solid'), an abbreviation of the expression *solidus nummus*, 'solid coin', the money paid to Roman soldiers during the time of the later Roman Empire. This consisted of coins made from substantial pieces of metal (even gold) rather than the flimsy bits of silver used hitherto.

A curious feature of modern English is that when we talk about a soldier's stock-in-trade, the guns and bullets he takes into battle with him, we refer to either 'munitions' (a sixteenth-century word) or 'ammunition' (a seventeenth-century word). The reason for the two similar yet distinctive words is as follows.

The Latin for a 'defensive wall' was *moenia*, which itself was related to the verb *munire*, 'to defend'. Over time the term *moenia* came to be applied not just to the fortifications but to anything which could be used to keep an invading army at bay – that is, weapons. By the Middle Ages the word had been adopted by the French, who used the collective derivative term *la munition* for weaponry of all kinds. But to many of the soldiers, understandably, *la munition* sounded like *l'ammunition*. By the time the words had made their way into English both forms were considered acceptable, so we now refer to either 'ammunition' or 'munitions' depending on the context.

> Our God and soldiers we alike adore
> Ev'n at the brink of danger; not before:
> After deliverance, both alike requited,
> Our God's forgotten and our soldiers slighted.
>
> FRANCIS CHARLES, 'Of Common Devotion' (1632)

Solicitor

The Latin derivation of this word has led to a surprising number of widely differing senses with which the word has been used in English throughout the centuries. In Ancient Rome the verb *sollicitare* meant 'to agitate' or 'to harass', but in Medieval Latin the word had modified somewhat and had come to mean 'to look after', 'to take care of'. This, in brief, probably explains why a man or woman 'harassing' a possible client, offering sex in exchange for payment, can be accused of 'soliciting' (since 1710), but if we are concerned about somebody we can be 'solicitous' for their well-being.

The Latin *sollicitare* was made up of two words: *sollus*, 'complete', 'entire', and *citus* (the past participle of *ciere*, a verb meaning 'to move', 'to set in motion'). This suggests that when the word 'solicitor' first entered English in the fifteenth century to mean 'agent' it reflected the hope of those who employed him that he would concentrate on 'getting things moving' to achieve the desired result as specified by the client. By the 1570s the word was being applied to legal practitioners in much the same way as it is today, but still retained the expectation of those paying the bill that he would 'agitate' on their behalf.

It was also about this time that 'solicitor' was applied to men who engaged in the promotion of the business affairs of others. There is still an overlap here as, although solicitors advise on everyday legal matters such as conveyancing and the drawing up of wills, they are also involved in offering advice to businesses.

Visitors from the UK to America have to be careful. In addition to being used in a legal context, the term 'solicitor' is also quite common as a description of what in the UK is often referred to as a 'door-to door' salesman.

> This supernatural soliciting
> Cannot be ill, cannot be good.
>
> WILLIAM SHAKESPEARE, *Macbeth* (1606), 1.3

Sorcerer

Sorcerers, along with witches and wizards, now feature mainly in fiction or in films and are frequently intended to be little more than an added ingredient in an entertaining narrative. But a mere few centuries ago things were very different and witchcraft was taken very seriously. During the English Civil War there was even a certain Matthew Hopkins (*c.* 1620–1647) operating in East Anglia and known unofficially as the Witchfinder General. His largely self-appointed role was to search high and low for witches and have them tried and executed on the flimsiest of evidence. Further north, in Lancashire, there was the dreadful episode in the 1600s when the so-called Pendle witches were condemned to death in Lancaster prison for virtually no reason at all, and certainly not for what today would qualify as 'evidence'.

Etymologically, the words 'witch' and 'wizard' are thought to be derived from the Indo-European root *wid*, meaning 'to know', so that witches and wizards were simply people who 'knew' things others did not know.

Sorcerers, whose talents overlapped with those of the witches and wizards, acquired their name from their ability to predict the fate of other people. In the fourteenth century 'sorcer', as it was originally spelled, entered English from the Medieval Latin *sortarius*, 'a teller of fortunes', itself a derivation of the Latin *sors*, 'fate', 'lot', 'fortune'. By the fifteenth century the spelling had altered to 'sorcerer' and additional abilities had been added to those thus described, including the power to conjure up evil spirits for malevolent purposes.

Until the Age of Enlightenment, when the application of reason began the long process of dispelling many of these superstitious beliefs, sorcerers and the like would have been described as 'weird' (such as the three witches in the opening scene of Shakespeare's *Macbeth*). This would not have been a reference to their strange or eccentric behaviour, a meaning the word has enjoyed only since the nineteenth century. Up until then, a 'weird' man or woman was somebody who could predict a person's *wyrd*, the Old English for 'fate'.

Spencer

Spencer (also Spenser) has been a fairly common surname in England since the thirteenth century, when it was more commonly encountered as *Le Despenser*. This was the Norman French trade description applied to the person responsible for the supervision and distribution of foodstuffs in a household. Ultimately, it was a term derived from the Latin *pendere*, 'to weigh', suggesting that the very first 'spencers' were household members whose duty it was to 'weigh out' the portions of food for the other occupants.

In medieval Scotland the term 'spencer' was used for the occupation which in England had become 'larderer'. This was the person charged with the running and supervision of the 'larder', later on a general food cupboard, but originally a room where meat was stored, particularly all the different cuts of meat from the pig. In Old French this room was called the *lardier*, a word derived from Medieval Latin *lardarium*, itself a derivation of *laridum*, the name the Ancient Romans gave to the fat off bacon. We have a descendant of this today in the modern French word *lardon*, often incorrectly translated as 'bacon'.

The Romans' word was a borrowing of the Greek word *larinos*, 'fat', related to another word, *laros*, meaning 'sweet' or 'tasty'.

Few houses nowadays are built with a room specifically called the 'pantry', but not so long ago few houses were built without one. Before the advent of fridges and

freezers, such small rooms, attached to the kitchen, were designed for storing food of just about any kind. Originally, however, the pantry was strictly for the storage of bread. It derives its name from Anglo-Norman *panetrie* and the Old French *paneterie*, from *panis*, the Latin for 'bread'.

> Here with a loaf of bread beneath the bough,
> A flask of wine, a book of verse – and Thou
> Beside me singing in the wilderness –
> And wilderness is paradise enow.
>
> EDWARD FITZGERALD, *The Rubaiyat of Omar Khayyam*
> (1859)

Spy

For many of us the typical spy is James Bond, the handsome, suave character, irresistible to women, who takes on the forces of evil almost single-handedly and always wins. Thus the world is saved from certain destruction and 007 can enjoy a relaxing vodka Martini (shaken not stirred) before reporting back to 'M' to be briefed on his next mission. But any serious book on the subject, written by people who have seen the inside of the world of espionage, will immediately dispel this image. The real 'James Bonds' are more likely to look like insurance salesmen, blend in with the background to the point of being virtually invisible, and possess no distinguishing features which would lead them to stand out from the crowd. Patience and powers of observation and deduction are more valuable attributes in the real world of espionage than sex appeal and an air of urbane sophistication.

The word 'espionage' as a description of the activities of spies was borrowed from the French in the eighteenth century, but the word 'spy' itself has been a feature of English for much longer. As a variant of 'espy' it has been used in English since the thirteenth century and is a relative of the German *spähen*, 'to peek'. The implication, therefore, is that our spies are just professionals constantly attempting to have 'a peek' at what other people are doing.

The immediate antecedent of these terms is the Latin *specere*, 'to observe', a word that has spawned a whole host of words commonly in use in English, including: 'spectator' (someone who watches), 'spectacle' (something to be watched) and 'species' (originally simply 'outward appearance').

The government bodies that oversee this country's spies are officially referred to as the 'Intelligence Services'. It is tempting to think that they are so-called because they only employ bright people. This may or may not be true, but the etymological connection is interesting.

The word 'intelligence' is derived from the Latin *intelligere*, 'to understand', which itself is a compound of *inter*, 'among', 'between', and *legere*, 'to select', 'to gather'. And this explains the two meanings we attribute to the word: the ability to gather information and process it, whether it be in a military or a civilian context.

Stationer

A stationer sells stationery from a stationary site. To find out why this should be so, we have to have a look at how the stationer's trade evolved over the centuries.

In the Middle Ages most selling took place from movable stalls which traders would set up early on market days or at fairs, and then, at the end of the day, dismantle again and convey home on carts. Stationers, however, were in a separate category; they were among the first people to have permanent sites, for which there are two main reasons. In the first place, stationers were not simply people who sold quills, ink pots and paper; they were more akin to what we would think of as a bookseller-cum-publisher. It was the stationer's responsibility to coordinate all those involved in the various stages of the publishing process: the bookbinders, the parchment makers, the illustrators, the scriveners and eventually the printers.

In the second place, stationers were more often than not licensed by the expanding universities and required to be on hand for easy access as and when advice was needed and consultation advisable concerning the publication of a document or book. The dons preferred not to wait for market day or the next fair.

The Medieval Latin for such a person was *stationarius*, a term which defined a professional who traded from a permanent site or 'station'. But it was not until the seventeenth century that the word 'stationer' acquired the meaning we attach to it today, and the stock-in-trade was not termed 'stationery' until the eighteenth.

The derivative verb for all these terms is the Latin *stare*, 'to stand'.

Stevedore

Until the 1950s, 'stevedore' was quite a common synonym for 'docker', 'dock worker' (in the USA usually referred to as a 'longshoreman'), a man whose job it was to help load and unload ships bringing imports into the country and exporting goods to all corners of the world. In some ports a clear distinction was made between a 'stevedore' and a 'docker'. The former worked in the holds and was considered a skilled worker with the understanding of how best to store goods so that they did not move around in choppy seas. The latter remained on the dockside and prepared the cargoes for loading.

But when containerization was introduced in the second half of the twentieth century, things changed. Now cargoes were loaded into huge containers on the dockside and then lifted onto, and stored on, the ships' decks. The need for stevedores to pack the holds diminished or disappeared.

The term 'stevedore' entered English in the late eighteenth century, borrowed from the Spanish *estibador*, a noun derived from the verb *estibar*, originally meaning 'to compress wool' and later 'to stow a cargo'. The Latin derivative verb was *stipare*, 'to press closely together', 'to compact', a verb which can trace its origins back to the Greek *steibein*, 'to trample underfoot'. So there is an etymological link here between the man cramming a ship's hold with cargo in the twentieth century and an Ancient Greek walking along a dirt road, 'compressing' the soil beneath his feet as he approaches his destination.

And the idea of 'cramming' or 'compacting' is seen in another derivative word frequently encountered in modern English: 'constipation'.

Many words commonly found in English originated in Spanish, including:

Siesta	midday nap, Spanish version of Latin *sexta*, 'sixth' (hour)
Chorizo	pork sausage
Armada	armed (force)
Matador	literally 'killer'
Cucaracha	Anglicized as 'cockroach'
Sombrero	'hat', literally 'shade maker'
Mosquito	little *mosca* or fly
Mojito	literally 'dripping wet'
Adiós	'Goodbye', literally 'to God'
Amigo	'friend', originally 'loved one'
Caballero	'sir', literally 'horseman'
Alligator	corruption of *el legarto*, 'the lizard'
Guerrilla	literally 'little *guerra*' or war

||||||||||||||||||||||||||||||||||||||||||||||||||||||||||||||||||||||||||||||||||||||||||||||||||||||||

Steward

The designation 'steward' spans a yawning gap in the social structure of society. At one end the term has been used since the fourteenth century to denote a senior officer of the royal household, and at the other a more lowly ship's officer responsible for the stores taken on-board before a voyage. We also find stewards today in charge of the catering in establishments such as golf clubs or helping with the organization of race meetings or even supporting the police when demonstrators march through big cities. But whatever the historical or contemporary role of the steward, the derivation of the term is the same – and, from a social point of view, very humble.

The Old English word from which the modern 'steward' is derived was *stig-weard*, comprising two distinct nouns, *stig* and *weard*. The former had quite a variety of meanings: it could designate a house, a hall or a pen in which the cattle were kept. The latter, *weard*, applied to just about anyone whose role was to protect other people or property, probably more recognizable in its modern spelling, 'ward'. For the Anglo-Saxons, a *stig-weard* was the man who protected the house, but by the thirteenth century the meaning had slid down the social ladder a little and applied to whoever took care of the pigs in a sty. And *stig-weard* gradually evolved into the spelling we have today, 'steward'.

The form 'Stewart' is a Scots form of the word and is first attested in the late fourteenth century, since when it has also become quite a common Christian name and surname. The alternative French spelling of Stuart was first used in 1429 and was the preferred form adopted by Mary, Queen of Scots (1542–1587).

In the late twelfth century another surname appeared in England: Granger, synonymous with 'steward'. This was based on the French term *grangier*, the man charged with looking after *une grange*, the French for a farmstead.

> Art any more than a steward? Dost thou think because thou art virtuous there shall be no more cakes and ale?
>
> WILLIAM SHAKESPEARE, *Twelfth Night* (1602), 2.3

Stockbroker

In the early days of banking, an ingenious way of keeping track of who was in debt to whom and for how much was to use what was known as a 'tally stick'. This cutting-edge piece of modern technology consisted of a length of wood along which a creditor and debtor would make little notches or cuts (*tailles* in Old French) at irregular intervals. The stick was then sliced lengthways and each party to the deal retained one half as an aide-memoire of the sums of money borrowed and lent. Later, as and when required, the two halves could be held together and the notches or *tailles* would be expected to match up perfectly. In other words, they were expected to 'tally'.

A further refinement to the tally-stick method of recording financial transactions was to have one half slightly longer than the other; this was known as 'the stock'. It was retained by the man who had lent the money, and he came to be known as the 'stockholder'. And it was this term that spawned expressions we easily recognize today: 'stock market', 'stockbroker, 'stocks and shares'.

In the fourteenth century a 'broker' was the general term for a commercial agent, although the word frequently carried undertones of sordid or dodgy business.

At a socially more acceptable level, the word was originally *brocour*, the Anglo-French for a small trader, particularly one who traded in wine. The derivative verb here is the Old French *brochier*, 'to pierce', a reference to the vintner's pleasant duty of having to thrust a pointed tool known as a *broche* into a keg or barrel of wine to release some of the contents for sampling before selling.

And the vintner's *broche* gave us another word commonly heard in modern English, 'brooch', an item of jewellery attached to clothing by means of a long, pointed pin.

> I love everything that's old: old friends, old times, old manners, old books, old wines.
>
> OLIVER GOLDSMITH, *She Stoops to Conquer* (1773)

Surveyor

In the early part of the fifteenth century the word 'surveyor' appeared in English, via Anglo-Norman, as a synonym for 'guard'. No doubt such a person would have been appointed by the lord of a manor, or at least someone in authority, to 'keep an eye' on his land, property or even people working for him. By the middle of the century the sense of the word had altered slightly and meant 'to examine the condition of', but by 1540 'to survey' was on the way to having the meaning we attach to it today, 'to take the linear measurements of an area of land'.

Now, of course, the surveyor is the person we rely on to combine the two earlier meanings from the fifteenth and sixteenth centuries: to examine a tract of land, carry out any required measurements and to assess the condition of any buildings on it.

The origin of the term is the Medieval Latin *supervidere*, which evolved from the Latin *super*, 'over', and *videre*, 'to see'. In the mid-1400s the English words themselves combined, giving 'to oversee' with exactly the same meaning as its Latin-based equivalent. But by the sixteenth century, the Latin combination of *super* and *videre* had produced yet another verb in English, 'to supervise'. So the situation now is that 'surveyor', 'overseer' and 'supervisor' are all variations on the same theme.

> I am monarch of all I survey,
> My right there is none to dispute
>
> WILLIAM COWPER, 'The Solitude
> of Alexander Selkirk' (1782)

Tailor

First recorded in English as a surname in Somerset in 1182, Tailor (alternatively spelled Taylor) is the fourth most common surname in the UK. As the definition of a profession, it made its appearance in English *c.* 1300 in the Anglo-Norman form of *taillour* or *tailour*, adopted and adapted from the Old French *tailleor*, which was a term for both a man who made clothes and a stonemason. If we consider that the derivative verb here was the Latin *taliare*, 'to cut', we see that the connection is not all that strange: one cuts cloth and the other cuts stone. This possibly led to a certain amount of confusion, so that by the Middle Ages the Medieval Latin for the man who produced clothing for the populace was defined more specifically as a *taliator vestium*, literally 'cutter of clothes'.

Although 'cutting' is the basic idea behind the term, the passage of time brought with it a considerable blurring of the edges concerning the evolution of the word. Broadly speaking, in modern English a 'tailor' is simply a person who makes clothes. In the trade, however, the 'tailor' is now the man or woman who sews together all the bits of cloth which have been 'cut out' by the 'cutter'. And historically there was a further confusion: in the Middle Ages a *taillour* measured his customers and produced the clothing to fit the individual, but clothes made to be sold 'off the peg' were produced by a 'clothier'. The 'bespoke' tailor (again, one who worked to order) appeared in the sixteenth century, the adjective being derived from the archaic use of the verb 'to bespeak', meaning 'to order in advance'.

The verb 'to tailor' did not appear until the 1660s, and its figurative use, as in 'tailor to one's needs', is not found before the 1940s.

The occupation of tailor has provided surnames in many countries, including:

German	Schneider, Schroeder, Schneiderman
Italian	Sarti
Hungarian	Szabo
Spanish	Sastre
Russian	Portnoy
Ukrainian	Kravchuk, Kravchenko
Greek	Raftēs
Dutch	Snijder

Tanner

The tanner plays a crucial role in the production of leather, and has done since time immemorial. In Anglo-Saxon times he was known as a *tannere*, a name derived from the Old English verb *tannian*, meaning 'to convert hide into leather by steeping it in tannin'. By about the year 900 the meaning of *tannere* had evolved a little so that in Medieval Latin the word applied to the man or woman who would dye leather in order to give it a specifically tawny (originally 'tanny') hue. The concept of 'tanning' something by leaving it out in the sun where it would turn a reddish-brown colour dates from only the sixteenth century.

A closely associated noun here is the medieval Latin *tannum*, the term for the bark which had been stripped off an oak tree, crushed into a powder and then mixed with water to produce 'tannin'. This magical liquid was then used for soaking the untreated hide, an important stage in the process of converting it into leather. But the original derivation of this word seems to be Celtic; the Breton term for an 'oak tree' is *tann*, etymologically related to the German *Tannenbaum*, 'fir tree'.

In the days when it was considered acceptable to administer corporal punishment, phrases such as 'I'll tan your hide' and 'you'll get a good hiding' were commonly heard. Such threats, dating from the seventeenth century, were a prediction of what was about to happen to a miscreant's skin when beaten with a stick; nowadays the only 'tanning' allowed is by exposure to the sun.

The person whose job it was to strip the bark off oak trees to provide the wherewithal for the tanning process to begin was known as a 'barker', but so close was the working relationship between a barker and a tanner that the titles became almost interchangeable for anybody who worked with animal hides. And both Tanner and Barker have been English surnames since the twelfth and thirteenth centuries respectively.

Tattooist

Recent years have seen an explosion in the popularity of the tattoo, and our high streets have seen an equivalent burgeoning of the 'office' where the tattooist plies his or her trade, the 'tattoo parlour'.

Archaeologists have found evidence of decorative body scarring from almost all over the ancient world, with perhaps the oldest example, found in the Alpine ice, dating back to around 3000 BCE. In modern Europe, it would seem, the man we have to thank for this kind of body art is none other than Captain James Cook, the eighteenth-century explorer. On his first voyage to the South Seas some of his crew were simultaneously surprised and delighted by the manner in which the natives adorned their bodies with pretty pictures and complex designs. Not to be outdone, they tried it on themselves (no doubt with help or guidance from the indigenous population), at the same time as adopting the Polynesian terminology for their newly acquired skill. At first they referred to the skin drawing as 'tattaow' or 'tattow' before settling on the spelling we recognize today. But whatever way the word is spelled, the derivation of it is the same: the Samoan and Tahitian word was *tatau*, which in Samoan was the verb 'to strike', giving us a fair indication of how the original drawings were applied to the skin.

Tattooing in Britain was for many years associated only with sailors and criminals, but in the 1870s the practice acquired a degree of popularity among a wider section of society. By 1894 it was deemed respectable enough, and therefore the demand for tattooists great enough, for a salon offering the service to open its doors in London, owned by the first professional tattoo artist, Sutherland Macdonald.

Taxi driver

It may be stating the obvious, but a taxi driver drives customers (usually known as 'fares') in a 'taxi' to wherever they want to go. And if the name by which this type of vehicle is known bears some resemblance to the 'taxes' (one of two certainties in life, the other being death) we all have to pay, it is no coincidence. Both words have come down to us via the same linguistic route.

'Taxi' is actually an abbreviation of the word 'taximeter cab', which first entered English in the early 1900s. It was a direct borrowing from the French, who had coined the word *taximètre* a few years before, the root of which is the word *taxe*, 'tariff', 'tax' or 'duty'. The basic idea was that the fare or 'tariff' would be calculated or 'measured' according to the distance travelled. The derivative French verb here is *taxer,* 'to tax', a descendant of the Latin *taxare*, meaning 'to charge'.

The second element in the word, 'cab', has an even more surprising history. Before the invention of the

internal combustion engine, all land transport was by horse-drawn vehicle of one type or another. In nineteenth-century France one such mode of conveyance was the *cabriolet*, which took its name from *cabriole*, 'a goat's leap', and the verb *cabrioler*, 'to leap in the air', a close relative of the Italian *capriolare*, 'to jump in the air', itself derived from *capriolo*, 'roebuck', and the Latin *caper*, meaning 'a goat'. And what linked a horse-drawn carriage with a goat?' The answer is: the springs. These lightweight carriages were so springy that, as soon as they began to move at a reasonable pace, they bounced up and down and made the passengers feel like cavorting goats.

||||||||||||||||||||||||||||||||||||||||||||||||||||||||||||||||||||||||||||||||||||||||||||||||||||

TAXICAB OR MINICAB?

In the UK a clear distinction is made between a 'taxicab' and a 'minicab'. The former may be hailed and hired by anyone walking along the street who feels the need to be taken to their destination with greater speed and in more comfort than shanks's pony can provide. On the other hand, if a 'minicab' is required, it has to be ordered in advance and the fare is then taken from where he or she is at the moment directly to the address stated when the order was placed.

Teacher

Schools (which, believe it or not, take their name from a Greek word meaning 'leisure time') are staffed by teachers. These are the people who take on the enormous task and responsibility of ensuring that the next generation of pupils will have the necessary skills and competences to face the world as they grow up. They have to be shown how to write, how to cope with mathematical calculations and, not least, how to behave as considerate members of society.

In Anglo-Saxon England the adult who taught children the rudiments of reading and writing or instructed them in Latin grammar would have been known as a *lǣrestre* or *lār-ēow*, based on *lǣran*, 'to teach', the verb which gave us the modern 'to learn' (German still has *Lehrer* for 'teacher'). At some time around the year 1300 the word 'teacher' found its way into English, but its primary meaning at the time was 'index finger', the finger with which we point to things or 'indicate' where they are. And this is a pretty good clue to the derivation of the word.

The derivative Old English verb *tǣcan* basically meant 'to point out', the Indo-European root here being *deik*, 'to show', a root which also produced 'digit', synonymous with finger, but also (from the fifteenth century) any number between 0 and 10, so-called because the most primitive form of counting is done on the fingers.

Etymology, then, suggests that by the early fourteenth century a 'teacher' was thought of as someone who instructed his or her charges by 'pointing out' facts, and 'showing the way' to achieving what was then considered a decent level of scholarship. And a century later he or she was also showing them how to count using their 'digits' or fingers.

Another cognate is the word 'token'. If we present someone with a 'token of our affection' we are, etymologically speaking, giving them a little gift to show our positive feelings towards them. And an 'apple for the teacher' completes the circle: it is a 'token' of gratitude for all the hard work the teacher has put in during term time as he or she 'pointed out' the way to academic success.

> O, she doth teach the torches to burn bright!
> It seems she hangs upon the cheek of night
> As a rich jewel in an Ethiope's ear –
> Beauty too rich for use, for earth too dear.
> WILLIAM SHAKESPEARE, *Romeo and Juliet* (1596?), 1.5

Telegraph boy

To today's younger generation, brought up on emails, mobile telephones, text messages, allowing instantaneous communication with people literally on the other side of the world, it must be incomprehensible that not so very long ago such easy contact was beyond the stuff of dreams.

As recently as the 1980s, the most common form of written communication was still the letter (handwritten or typed) or, for urgent messages, the telegram.

In comparison with the speed of today's communications this was cumbersome and time-consuming, but the only way of getting in touch when there was no telephone available or the recipient was miles away or possibly on the other side of the world. The sender would go to the nearest post office, write out the message on a dedicated form, hand it to the person behind the counter, who would arrange for it to be sent by telegraph to the post office nearest the recipient's address. It would then be handed to a telegraph boy, who would get on his bike and ride to the specified location and hand it to the addressee.

In the First and Second World Wars the telegraph boy walking up the drive or standing on a doorstep could strike fear and dread in the heart of the householder; telegrams in those days frequently brought news that a loved one had been killed on a far-flung field of battle or was 'missing presumed dead'. In the 1950s the telegraph boy was still a frequent sight, although now a lesser percentage of his signature yellow envelopes contained disturbing news. It had become a tradition, for instance, for telegraph boys to deliver greetings telegrams to the happy couple from relatives who could not attend a wedding. By the 1980s the telephone had become so easily accessible that the telegraph service in the UK was terminated after more than 130 years.

The word 'telegraph' is pure Greek. It is made up of the adverb *tēle*, meaning 'at a distance', and the verb *graphein*, 'to write', so that the literal meaning of the word is 'to write at a distance'. And when the 'telegraph boy' delivered the 'telegram' things had moved into the arcane realms of the Greek verbal system; *gramma* was a past passive form of *graphein* and so meant 'that which has been written'.

Tobacconist

In the not too distant past almost every high street in Britain boasted a 'sweets and tobacco' shop and many had a specialist tobacconist selling pipes, pipe tobacco, cigars, cigarettes, snuff and all the paraphernalia that the serious smoker needed. But now the situation is quite different; as the number of smokers has decreased dramatically, so has the availability of tobacco products. And the principal reason for the falling popularity of the habit was the discovery that tobacco smoking causes cancer and a host of other nasty health problems.

But tobacco was not always thought of as harmful. When the plant was introduced from South America to Europe in 1559 it was considered a medicinal herb and something of a panacea for everything from gout to toothache and even cancer. According to some sources, when the Great Plague struck London in 1665, the pupils at Eton College were instructed to smoke a pipe-full of tobacco every morning as it was believed the smoke prevented 'bad air' and guarded against the spread of disease.

The word itself is thought to be derived from the Spanish or Portuguese *tabaco* (taken straight from a Caribbean language called Taino), the native word for the plant. Another possibility is that the original was *tabago*, the native term for the pipe in which the tobacco (*cohiba*) was smoked. Yet another theory is that the word is actually based on the Arabic *tubbaq*, applied by the Arabs to various herbs since the ninth century.

The term 'tobacconist' underwent a complete reversal of meaning after it was first used in England in the sixteenth century. It was originally applied to people who put tobacco in their pipes and smoked it; it was not until a century later that the man or woman who made a living from selling tobacco products became universally known as a 'tobacconist'.

One of the harmful ingredients in tobacco, nicotine, takes its name from a certain Jean Nicot, a French diplomat, who is credited with introducing the leaf into France in 1560.

Travel agent

As the name suggests, a travel agent is someone who will act for us, offering help and advice and taking care of most of the arrangements when we wish to 'travel' somewhere. He or she is the person who will make the journey as pleasant as possible and help us avoid all the hitches and glitches, problems and stress, that any trip, however brief, can entail. In other words, the travel agent will normally do all he or she can to remove the difficulties which could make our journey an arduous task and sheer hard work rather than a pleasure to be savoured and enjoyed. And this explains the derivation of the word 'travel'.

For the origin of the word, we have to make our own journey back through time to Ancient Rome and the enlightened civilization that gave us wonderful literature, sculpture, architecture and much of our legal system. It was, however, also a society that depended on slavery for much of its commercial and military success as it spread its influence out through vast tracts of the known world.

Slavery, of course, is a cruel system in any society and the Romans were no paragons of virtue when it came to managing their slaves. If a slave was deemed not to be working hard enough, a Roman soldier would beat him or her with an instrument of torture known as a *trepalium* (a kind of truncheon made by binding three sticks together), from the words *tres*, 'three', and *palus*, 'stake'.

Eventually, *trepalium* morphed into the word for 'work' in several European languages: *trabajo* in Spanish, *travaille* in French, 'travail' in thirteenth-century English. By the fourteenth century 'travail' in English had acquired the additional meaning of 'going on a journey' or, as we would now say, 'travelling'.

> I never travel without my diary. One should always have something sensational to read in the train.
>
> OSCAR WILDE, *The Importance of Being Earnest* (1895)

Treasurer

The treasurer in any organization is the man or woman appointed to look after the finances. To put it another way, he or she is responsible for taking care of the organization's 'treasure', which in the modern world includes cash in the bank, property and other assets. All this is far more mundane than the eighteenth-century pirates' 'treasure chest', brim-full with rubies, diamonds and gold, buried beneath the sands on some remote Pacific island. However, the etymological connection between the two concepts is very strong.

The word 'treasurer' was first used in English in the late thirteenth century when it borrowed the Old French word *tresorer*, developed from the twelfth-century noun *tresor*, taken from the Latin *thesaurus*, and ultimately from the Greek *thēsauros*. The derivative Greek verb here was *thēsaurizein*, meaning 'to store up', 'to lay in store', but not solely in a financial context. A farmer on the outskirts of Ancient Athens would keep a *thēsauros* of fruit and pickled vegetables to see his family through the winter; and if he had any valuables he would have placed them in another *thēsauros* or special casket for safekeeping. Ultimately, all these words derive from the Greek verb *tithemi*, 'I put', which brings us back to the pirates who simply 'put' their no doubt ill-gotten gains in a safe place in the sand for future recovery and collection.

Of course, in modern English we also use the word 'thesaurus' to mean a specialized kind of dictionary which lists a word's synonyms and antonyms as well as its definition. When it was first used in the sixteenth century the word could mean a dictionary or encyclopaedia; the current meaning dates only from 1852 and the publication of *Roget's Thesaurus of English Words and Phrases*. And for many a writer, Peter Roget's magnum opus has certainly been an indispensable 'treasure chest' of linguistic information neatly 'stored' between the covers.

> But the privilege and pleasure
> That we treasure beyond measure
> Is to run on little errands for the Ministers of State!
>
> W.S. GILBERT, *The Gondoliers* (1899)

Tycoon

Some time after the First World War the epithet 'tycoon' found its way into Britain and was applied to high-powered captains of industry. Earlier, in the nineteenth century, it had been a term borrowed by European visitors to Japan, but applied to Japanese warlords. 'Tycoon' is the anglicized version of the Japanese *taikun*, meaning 'great lord'.

The person we have to thank mainly for the entry of this word into English was a certain Commodore Perry (1794–1858) of the American navy. For over two hundred years Japan had been closed to the outside world as the shoguns (hereditary commanders-in-chief of the Japanese army) feared that too much contact with other nations, particularly those of the West, would have a pernicious effect on an ancient culture which had so long character-ized the Land of the Rising Sun. A year before his death in 1858, Commodore Perry was instrumental in persuading, with the help of a few unsubtle threats involving gunboats, the Shogun of Tokukawa to sign the Convention of Kanagawa, initiating trade between the two nations and effectively ending Japan's years of isolation.

When he returned to the USA in 1857, Commodore Perry brought the Japanese term *taikun* with him and it seems to have caught on among the populace. In fact, the title was soon being applied to the president, Abraham Lincoln, albeit in a playful or jocular manner, by a couple of his aides. But it soon spread to other sections of society to describe industrialists and powerful businessmen, and just over half a century later it was a term generally accepted in the English-speaking world.

IIIIIIIIIIIIIIIIIIIIIIIIIIIIIIIIIIIIIIIIIIIIIIIIIIIIIIIIIIIIIIIIIIIIIIIIIIIIIIIIIIIIIIIIIIIIIIIIIIIIIIIII

Other Japanese words adopted into English
(with literal translations):

Judo	'the gentle way'
Ju-jitsu	'the gentle technique'
Tsunami	'harbour wave'
Karaoke	'empty orchestra'
Origami	'fold paper'
Tofu	'sour beans'
Sumo	'striking one another'
Ninja	'spy'
Kimono	'thing for wearing'
Zen	'meditation'
Emoji	'picture character'
Karate	'empty hand'
Kamikaze	'Divine wind'

IIIIIIIIIIIIIIIIIIIIIIIIIIIIIIIIIIIIIIIIIIIIIIIIIIIIIIIIIIIIIIIIIIIIIIIIIIIIIIIIIIIIIIIIIIIIIIIIIIIIIIIII

Typist

In the 1950s, when society still thought in terms of 'boys' jobs' and 'girls' jobs', one of the main occupations into which girls were steered when they left school was that of 'typist', of either the 'shorthand' or 'copy' variety. And there was no shortage of demand for those who qualified with good typing skills; almost every office, business or commercial institution throughout the land

resounded from nine till five with the clackety-clack of at least a couple, and possibly dozens, of typewriters, depending on the size of the organization. But those days are no more. Since the advent of the personal computer in the 1990s, the need for a dedicated 'typing pool' (as the 'girls' were collectively known) has vanished. Emails have largely taken the place of the typed letter; texting has almost become the norm for brief communications; and full-length letters can be produced on a screen by the initiator before he or she presses a button and commands the printer to spew out as many copies as are required.

The term 'typist' was first applied to typewriter operators in 1844. It was a noun based on the Greek verb *tuptein* (or *typtein*), meaning 'to strike', 'to make an impression on', and the connection is obvious: a 'typist' in the early days had to give the keys quite a thump if the machine's striking arm was to make any kind of impression on the paper.

The noun 'type' as a synonym of 'kind' is from the very same Greek root. The noun *tupos* (or *typos*) referred to a 'figure', 'image' or 'form', produced by striking metal or clay, whether deliberately or not, and leaving a mark or an impression. So, when we talk about a person being of such and such a 'type' we are metaphorically referring to their 'stamp' – that is, distinguishing marks or individual characteristics.

Umpire

In English, a person who is called in to settle a dispute between two opposing parties has since the fifteenth century been known as an 'umpire'. But the spelling is due to what linguists refer to as 'metanalysis', meaning that, strictly speaking, the word should be 'a numpire' rather than 'an umpire'. This feature of English can be seen in other examples, such as 'an apron', which was originally 'a napron', and 'an orange', derived as it is from the Arabic *naranj*, which should be 'a norange'.

'Numpire' reflects the Old French *nompere* or *nonper*, based on the Latin *non*, 'no', and *par*, 'equal', meaning 'not equal' and 'odd number'. The relevance here to the modern meaning is that if two sides cannot agree, a third person is brought into the argument, thus making an 'odd number' attempting to find an agreement or compromise. In such a situation, the third person will be expected to side with one of the adversaries and thus the danger of a split decision will be avoided.

The practice of resorting to an umpire in cases of dispute was originally confined to the law courts. But eventually it spread to other walks of life, including sport, and in 1714 the title 'umpire' was first recorded as applying to the official who decided who was the winner in a wrestling match. Nowadays, an 'umpire' is more usually found on tennis courts or cricket pitches; wrestlers are judged to have won or lost by the 'referee'.

The Latin *par* also found its way into English in other contexts. It was first used in golf in 1898; from 1928 the expression 'par for the course' found acceptance colloquially as a synonym for 'average' or 'as might be expected'. And, of course, anyone not performing as well as he or she normally does can be described as being 'below par'.

Undertaker

Nowadays, an 'undertaker' is universally understood to be the person who 'undertakes' to perform all those duties associated with a funeral. But this interpretation of the word has applied only since the 1690s; previously, an 'undertaker' was simply a man or woman who was contracted to perform or 'undertake' whatever duty or service was required. In the late seventeenth century the term 'funeral undertaker' entered the language; eventually the adjective was dropped and the noun acquired the meaning we associate with it today.

The word 'funeral' entered English as an adjective in the fourteenth century but, curiously, it was not used as a noun until the sixteenth. Both the adjective and the noun are derived from the Medieval Latin *funeralia*, in turn derived from the Latin *funus*, 'corpse'.

Closely connected with a funeral, of course, is the word 'hearse', which has a fascinating origin. It is derived from the Latin *hirpex*, meaning 'a large rake', and the Old French *herse*, 'a harrow'. At some point somebody had the idea of taking a harrow, normally used for raking the hard earth, turning it upside down and using it for conveying the dear departed to the church and then to the place of burial. But there was a further development: it occurred to another bright spark that pushing candles down onto the upturned spikes resulted in a makeshift candelabrum which could, on dark winter days, shed a little light on the proceedings. And this brilliant idea meant that, for the family and friends of the deceased, the obsequies would perhaps be a little less 'harrowing'.

Valet

In America, if we arrive at an airport and want somebody to park our car while we fly off to some distant destination, we call for a 'parking valet'. In Britain, if we decide to have the interior of our car professionally cleaned, we now arrange for it to be 'valeted'. Both of these usages of the word are far removed from its original meaning.

Since the sixteenth century it has been used to mean a 'gentleman's gentleman' – a personal servant of a male member of the British upper classes. It is a word derived from the Old French *valet* or *vaslet*, a borrowing of the

Medieval Latin *vassalus* and *vassus*, both of which meant 'servant'.

But this is far from the end of the story. An alternative of the Old French word was *varlet*, which as late as the mid-fifteenth century meant nothing more than 'attendant to a knight'. However, by the 1540s 'varlet' had become synonymous with 'rogue' or 'ne'er-do-well', no doubt as a reflection of what some of the knights' assistants got up to when they were not at their masters' beck and call.

Yet another closely related word is 'vassal'. In the fourteenth century this was the term for a tenant who pledged fealty to his lord or the monarch, in exchange for certain privileges, such as being able to occupy an estate and behave more or less as he wished within its confines.

And this is where the etymological trail follows a surprising route. 'Vassal' was, as we have seen, derived from Medieval Latin, but this was related to an ancient Celtic word resembling *wasso*, denoting a youth or young man and directly related to the modern Welsh *gwas*, meaning both 'servant' and 'lad'.

> In short he was a perfect cavaliero,
> And to his very valet seem'd a hero.

LORD BYRON, Beppo (1817)

Ventriloquist

Long before ventriloquists began entertaining people with their unusual skills in the early eighteenth century, the ability to 'throw one's voice' was considered on a par with witchcraft. In fact, in the Middle Ages it was not unknown for women skilled in the art to be burned at the stake, as they were deemed to be in communication with the Devil.

The association between ventriloquy (as ventriloquism was originally called) and the black arts may seem odd to us, but in Ancient Greece it was firmly believed that the various noises emanating from the ventriloquist's stomach (which we would probably put down to a poor or overactive digestive system) were the voices of the dead attempting to get in touch with the living. And the Greeks, who took such matters very seriously, attributed the additional gift of clairvoyance to those blessed with, or plagued by, troublesome gastric juices. At the Temple of Apollo at Delphi they even had a priestess, Pythia, a known *gastromyth* or 'stomach speaker', who foretold the future. The only problem was that she did so in riddles and left it up to the 'client' to try to interpret what she had actually said and to draw his or her own conclusions.

Gastromyth is made up of two Greek words, *gastēr*, 'stomach', and *mythos*, 'speech', so that the word literally means something along the lines of 'stomach speaking'. This was translated literally into Modern Latin, using the more or less equivalent words *venter*, 'belly', and *loqui*, 'to speak', and the combination produced *ventriloquium*, the forerunner of the modern English 'ventriloquist'.

> Drink no longer water, but use a little wine for
> thy stomach's sake and thine often infirmities.
>
> TIMOTHY 5:23

Vet

Until the 1520s the man or woman who looked after our animals for us when they were sick or had suffered an accident and needed medical attention was known by the term 'dog leech'. This was a description that had survived from Anglo-Saxon times and was based on the word 'dog' and the Old English for 'physician', *lǣce*. *Lǣce* or 'leech' had been the usual word for any medical practitioner for centuries, but by the seventeenth its use was being restricted to those professionals who offered their services solely to animals.

Also in the seventeenth century, another adjective appeared on the scene: 'veterinarian', coined by the polymath Sir Thomas Browne (1605–1682), who by training, qualifications and profession was a medical doctor. By the 1640s this had become a noun, so that 'a veterinarian' was gaining popularity as the normal determinant for anyone treating sick animals. In 1862 the first use was recorded of the abbreviated form we recognize today, 'vet'.

There is some discussion among etymologists over the exact derivation of the word; as things stand, the only point on which they all agree is that the derivative language is Latin.

The Latin word *veterinarius*, as an adjective, meant 'relating to beasts of burden'; as a noun it defined a 'cattle doctor'. A related noun is *veterinum*, meaning 'a beast of burden'. All are directly connected to the adjective *vetus*, simply meaning 'old'. The usual explanation for the link between these terms is that it was perhaps the 'experienced' (rather than 'aged') cattle who were considered mature enough to withstand the arduous life of a beast of burden.

The other theory is that *veterinarius* is in fact derived from the verb *vehere* (the verb that gave us our word 'vehicle'), 'to carry', 'to convey', suggesting that the original 'vets' confined their attention and expertise to draught animals.

Vintner

In the late fourteenth or early fifteenth century 'wine merchants' acquired an alternative title: vintner. This was an altered version of the Anglo-French word *vinetier*, who was both a purveyor of wines and the man who harvested the grapes. The Latin source of these words was *vinetum*, 'a vineyard', and *vinum*, wine.

But this was not the end of the story. The words in many European languages, such as French *vin*, English 'wine', Spanish and Italian *vino*, Russian *vinó*, and even Irish *fíon* and Welsh *gwin*, are all descended from, or related to, the Ancient Greek *oinos* and the Archaic Greek *woinos*. So it would appear that wine merchants or vintners have been lubricating convivial gatherings with their merchandise (playfully christened 'bottled poetry' by Robert Louis Stevenson) since ancient times.

Of course, the most usual source of wine is the grape, a word whose etymology is directly connected with the manner in which it is harvested. It was adopted into English in the thirteenth century from the Old French *grape*, meaning a 'bunch' or 'bunch of grapes'. This was derived from the verb *graper*, 'to grasp', 'to catch with a *grappe*' or hook.

Many proverbs and expressions involving wine have come down to us through the ages. One such is 'a good wine needs no bush', bequeathed to us by Shakespeare in *As You Like It*. The sense of the quotation is that if a thing is good enough it needs no advertising, but to understand the significance of the 'bush' we have to consider a social convention of the time. Owners of establishments that offered wine for

sale frequently displayed a bush or branch (often of ivy) outside the door to indicate that refreshments were to be had within. Presumably, if the wine was of good quality, the tavern's reputation would spread abroad and business would flourish even if the plant disappeared.

Wine is sunlight held together by water.

GALILEO GALILEI (1564–1642)

Water diviner

Dowsers (a seventeenth-century word of unknown origin) probably never think of themselves as being god-like, but the etymology of their more official title suggests that in the dim and distant past other people thought that they were. 'Water diviner' suggests that they were thought to have the powers of 'divination' (a word with distinctly theological connections), which would assist them as they used a forked twig and intuition to detect water underground.

'To divine', meaning to possess an almost supernatural ability to foretell the future, was adopted into English in the fourteenth century from the Old French *deviner*, 'to predict'. This was a derivation of the Latin *deus*, 'god', with its derivative adjective *divus*, 'god-like', and the verb *divinare*, 'to prophesy', a talent which, the word suggests, was closely associated with a divinity but denied to lesser mortals. The use of the adjective 'divine' in English to describe something wonderful dates from the late fifteenth century.

'Water' in Old English was *wæter*, and both this and its modern equivalent are closely related to the German *Wasser*, Dutch *water* and even the Russian *vodá*. Further connections are the Russian word *vódka* and the Gaelic *uisge*, also 'water' and found in the expression *uisge beatha*, literally 'water of life' but probably more recognizable to English speakers as 'whisky'.

And the Indo-European root *wed, which produced 'water' and its cognates in other languages, also gave us the words 'wet' and 'winter'.

> May you, may Cam and Isis preach it long!
> The Right Divine of Kings to govern wrong.
>
> ALEXANDER POPE, *The Dunciad* (1728)

Weaver

The surnames Weaver, Webb, Webber, Webster all share the same etymological derivation and define what were originally trades. What is probably generally not realized is that, because the names are now so common and gender-neutral, sight has been lost of the fact that the term 'webster', as a trade, applied only to women. In the Middle Ages a 'webster' was simply the female equivalent of a 'weaver' or 'webber' who wove cloth for a living. As surnames, they have all existed in English with one spelling or another since the middle of the thirteenth century.

The immediate antecedent of the word is basically Germanic, coming as it does from a supposed Proto-Germanic verb *weban*, used to describe the action of interlacing yarn.

The art of weaving, however, is not peculiar to men and women attempting to make an honest living. There are plenty of examples in the animal world of creatures that demonstrate an inherited, instinctive ability to weave: there is, for example, the 'weaver bird', so-called because of the ingenious way in which it can weave twigs together to make a nest.

In the insect world, there is the 'wasp', which, along with words in other languages such as *vespa* (Latin and Italian), *wesp* (Dutch), *Wespe* (German), is derived from the Indo-European root *webh*, meaning 'to weave'. Our observant ancestors all recognized wasps' ability to weave delicate structures within their nests.

But the arch-weaver has to be the spider. It takes its name from the Old English *spinnan*, 'to spin' (and is therefore related to 'spinster'), and the result of the time it spends spinning is the immensely strong yet flexible 'cobweb'. In Middle English this was known as a *coppeweb*, meaning literally 'a web of a *coppe*', originally an old word for 'head', but later also a 'spider'. And this was part of the Old English for 'spider', *ātorcoppe*, literally 'poison head'.

Oh, what a tangled web we weave,
When first we practise to deceive!

SIR WALTER SCOTT, Marmion (1808)

Wedding planner

Not so very long ago, when a young couple decided to get married, the parents (traditionally the bride's) took care of most, if not all, of the arrangements. But now it is rapidly becoming the norm to hire a wedding planner who will take all (or most) of the stress and worry out of arranging the big day.

In late Anglo-Saxon England the normal word for what we call a 'wedding' was *weddung*, closely related to another word, *wedd*, meaning 'pledge'. So, basically, the wedding ceremony occurred when two people made a 'pledge' to live together in a state of wedded bliss and procreate. *Wedd* was related to the Old High German *wetton*, also meaning 'pledge' and cognate with the Latin *vas* (genitive *vadis*), 'surety', 'bail'. Coincidentally, when a couple 'get engaged' they employ another verb based on the concept of a solemn promise: the root of the word, *gage*, is a fourteenth-century French import also meaning 'pledge'.

But Old English also had another word for marriage, *brīdelope*, literally 'bridal run', a reference to the young wife 'running' off to her new home after the ceremony. In the seventeenth century yet another, very similar, word appeared in English, 'elope', which until recently was what a young couple might do if the girl's father refused to give her permission to marry. Originally, however, the sense of the word was slightly different: it referred to a young wife running away with her lover if she was unhappy living with her husband. And 'husband', which in Old English was *hūsbonda*, was acquired from Old Norse, which had *husbondi*, comprising two elements, *hus*, 'house', and *bondi*, the present participle of the verb *bua*, 'to dwell'. So, literally, a 'husband' is a man 'dwelling in a house' with his *wyf* or 'woman'.

The state of being married is either 'wedlock' or 'marriage'. The latter entered English around the year 1300, from the Old French *mariage*, a word derived from the Latin *maritare*, 'to give in marriage'. But *maritare* was also the verb used when binding vines to trees, a practice presenting us with a rather romantic metaphor. This is enhanced by the sixteenth-century expression 'honeymoon', the 'month' after a wedding when the kisses are still as sweet as 'honey'.

> [M]en are April when they woo, December when they wed. Maids are May when they are maids, but the sky changes when they are wives.
>
> WILLIAM SHAKESPEARE, *As You Like It* (1599?), 4.1

White van man

Depending on our point of view (and immediate needs) the 'man with a van' can be a saint or a sinner. If we have a few bulky loads that need transporting from one place to another at a reasonable cost, the entrepreneurial young man with his own transport (which just happens to be white) could fit the bill nicely. On the other hand, these vehicles have been used by less responsible members of society for criminal activities as they know the police might find such unmarked vehicles difficult to trace. Either way, the 'white van man' seems here to stay for the foreseeable future.

The word 'van' is an abbreviated form of 'caravan', even though it might bear only a passing resemblance to what we alternatively call a 'mobile home'. And caravans of this type first became popular in the UK in the 1930s.

In the sixteenth century, however, the word conveyed a very different image. It referred to a company of

people and their camels, gathered together for reasons of security and self-protection, undertaking an arduous journey across one of the world's deserts. Alternatively, it could also define a fleet of Turkish ships crossing the sea in close formation, no doubt once again as a means of making a potential attacker think twice. And the dual imagery of this word probably explains the apparent confusion when we talk of the camel as being the 'ship of the desert'.

The French used the word *caravane* as early as the thirteenth century, having borrowed it from the Arabs during the Crusades. But it was not originally an Arabic word; it was adopted by the Arabs from the Persian *kārwān*, used to describe a group of people travelling across a desert. And the consensus of opinion among etymologists is that *kārwān* is related to the Sanskrit *karabha*, meaning 'camel', which leads us on to a fascinating connection. 'Camel' is related to the Greek *kamēlos* and the Hebrew/Phoenician *gamal*, which is probably related to the Arabic *jamala*, meaning 'to carry', 'to transport'.

If this connection is correct, it completes the circle and brings us right back to the role of today's 'white van man'.

Wigmaker

For one reason or another, men and women have been making and wearing wigs for hundreds, if not thousands, of years. Historians have evidence that natural hair was enhanced artificially in Ancient Greece, Rome, Assyria, Egypt and various other places, sometimes to show wealth or importance and sometimes to disguise the relentless approach of partial or total baldness. The cosmetic and psychological importance of our 'crowning glory' has been recognized in all societies throughout history.

And where we have wigs we also have to have wig-makers, and as the popularity of wigs increased so did the profession of wigmaker. In France a Wigmakers' Guild was established in 1665, a reflection of how popular the practice of wig wearing was becoming. Charles II of England (r. 1660–85) fell for its charms during his period of exile in France, and on his return to England did much to popularize the fashion among his courtiers and the upper echelons of society.

The term 'wig' is a seventeenth-century abbreviation of the longer 'periwig' (thought to have been first used in English by Shakespeare in his play *Two Gentlemen of Verona*, written between 1589 and 1593), a corruption of the French word *perruque*, which was borrowed directly from the Italian *perruca* or *parruca* and originally meant 'a [natural] head of hair'.

A less than total covering of the head, designed to cover a bald spot, is the 'toupée', which made its way into English in 1727. It was another borrowing from France, where the word *toupet* (the diminutive form of *top*, the Old French for 'tuft' or 'topknot') meant 'forelock'. Perhaps surprisingly, this was not originally designed to hide unwanted baldness; it was simply an artificial addition to what nature had provided and was nothing more than a fashion accessory.

> [I]t offends me to the soul to hear a robustious periwig-pated fellow tear a passion to tatters, to very rags, to split the ears of the groundlings,* who for the most part are capable of nothing but inexplicable dumb shows and noise.
>
> WILLIAM SHAKESPEARE, *Hamlet* (1599–1602?), 3.2

---

* 'Groundlings' were the members of the audience who stood in the theatre pit to watch a play.

Wright

Apart from being a common surname, this word has ceased to exist independently in modern English and is only found in compound nouns such as 'cartwright' (a maker of carts), 'wheelwright' (a maker of wheels), wainwright (a maker of wains, or carts), 'arkwright' (a maker of chests), 'shipwright' (a shipbuilder) and millwright (originally a maker of the parts that kept flour mills in good working order).

The word that does not sit very well here is 'playwright'. It evokes a more cerebral occupation than its physically demanding counterparts with their emphasis on producing artefacts (usually made of wood) of practical use to society as opposed to entertainment. And for the reason behind this apparent anomaly we have to go all the way back to the dramatists of the seventeenth century. Ben Jonson (1572–1637), who wrote plays but always referred to himself as a poet, first used the term in 1605, suggesting that writers who produced mere potboilers for the theatre were on a par with the 'wrights' or labourers who toiled all day in their workshops. Such a dismissive and pejorative attitude persisted until the early nineteenth century.

And 'workshop' is a convenient lead-in to the derivation of the word 'wright'. In Old English is was *wryhta* or *wyrhta*, of West Germanic origin and related to the verb *wyrcan*, 'to work'. Both the noun and the verb can be traced back to the Indo-European root *werg*, which makes them cognate with the Ancient Greek *ergon* and the Archaic Greek *wergon*, 'work'.

||||||||||||||||||||||||||||||||||||||||||||||||||||||||||||||||||||||||||||||||||||||||||||||||||

Some famous Wrights in history:

Frank Lloyd Wright (1869–1959) Architect who designed the Guggenheim Museum in New York. Famous for his theory of 'organic architecture'.

Joseph Wright (1734–1797) British painter noted for his industrial and scientific subjects, such as *An Experiment on a Bird in the Air Pump* (1767).

Joseph Wright (1855–1930) British etymologist.

Judith Arundel wright (1915–2000) Australian poet and critic.

Richard Wright (1908–1960) Novelist and short-story writer. Best known for his novel *Native Son* (1940).

Wilbur Wright (1867–1912) and Orville Wright (1871–1948) American aviation pioneers who designed the first powered aircraft in 1903.

||||||||||||||||||||||||||||||||||||||||||||||||||||||||||||||||||||||||||||||||||||||||||||||||||

Zoologist

The word 'zoologist' was adopted into English in about the year 1660 as a definition of someone who made a scientific study of the animal kingdom. It was based on the Modern Latin *zoologia*, 'the study of animals'. This in turn was a direct borrowing of the Greek *zōē*, meaning 'life' (and also the source of the name Zoe), and its derivative *zōion*, an 'animal'. Other words in modern English containing the same Greek root include 'zoo' (a place where animals can be observed), the 'zodiac' (division of the year into sections, each represented by an animal) and 'protozoa' (literally 'first life', a term defining the most primitive of life forms.) But the Greeks also had another word for 'life', *bios*, which spawned a host of words in English such as 'biology' (the study of life) and 'biologist' (the occupation of somebody who spends his or her working days studying various forms of life). So, the professions of 'zoologist' and 'biologist' are etymologically synonymous.

Early in the fourteenth century the word 'animal' made its way into English; by the early seventeenth century it had virtually ousted the term 'beast', a derivative of the Latin *bestia*. And the basis of 'animal' was the Latin *anima*, which could mean 'a current of air', 'breath' and, after the word was adopted into Christianity, 'soul'. The Indo-European root at play here is *ane*, 'to breathe', the same root that gave us words such an 'anemone' (a flower that opens only when there is a breath of wind) and 'unanimous' (of one mind or soul).

Man is the only animal that blushes. Or needs to.
MARK TWAIN, *Following the Equator* (1897)

GLOSSARY
OF TERMS

ANCIENT GREEK The Greek spoken and written by the classical authors about the fifth century BCE.

ANGLO-NORMAN A combination of English and Norman French spoken and written in England after the Norman Conquest of 1966.

ARCHAIC GREEK An older form of the language dating from approximately the time of Homer, i.e. eighth century BCE.

CELTIC An Indo-European group of languages which include Welsh, Scots and Irish Gaelic, Cornish, Manx and Breton.

COGNATE Indicating that two words share a common ancestor and not that one is descended from the other.

GOTHIC A well-documented east Germanic language, with the oldest extant written records dating from the fourth century CE. It was, to all intents and purposes, extinct by the ninth century.

HINDI Indo-European language spoken in northern India and closely related to Urdu. It is the official language of India.

INDO-EUROPEAN Essentially a reconstructed form of the assumed parent language of most of the languages spoken in Europe and northern India. By convention, it is usual to precede reconstructed word forms with an asterisk to indicate that the form is hypothetical. It is sometimes referred to as Proto-Indo-European.

LATE LATIN The form of Latin spoken and written between the third and sixth centuries CE.

LATIN Sometimes also termed 'classical Latin', the language of Ancient Rome from 75 BCE to the third century CE.

MEDIEVAL LATIN Current between the fifth and fifteenth centuries, it was a language of communication between scholars, lawyers and men of letters.

METANALYSIS The splitting of a word so that the first letter becomes part of the preceding word – e.g. 'an orange' for an original 'a norange'. Formerly termed 'misdivision'.

MIDDLE FRENCH Flourished in Europe from the fourteenth century until the early seventeenth.

MIDDLE ENGLISH The language of Chaucer. Basically Old English heavily influenced by Norman French.

MIDDLE LOW GERMAN Also known as Middle Saxon, it served as a lingua franca in northern Europe during the period of the Hanseatic League (c. 1300–1600).

MODERN LATIN A form of Classical Latin resurrected for use in scholarly works. Commonly used from the late fourteenth century to 1900 for scientific nomenclature, particularly in the fields of botanical and zoological taxonomy.

OLD ENGLISH Now the preferred term for what used to be called Anglo-Saxon. It was spoken and written through most of England from the mid-fifth to the mid-twelfth century. Related to the Scandinavian languages, German and Icelandic.

OLD FRENCH Romance language spoken in Europe from the ninth to the fourteenth century CE.

OLD HIGH GERMAN The earliest stage in the development of German, dating from c. 700 to 1050 CE.

OLD NORSE Northern Germanic language spoken mainly in Scandinavia between the eighth and fourteenth centuries.

PROTO-GERMANIC A reconstructed parent language of the Germanic and Scandinavian languages. It is thought to have been spoken *c.* 500 BCE.

PROVENÇAL A version of French spoken mainly in the South of France but also in parts of Italy and Monaco. According to tradition, this was the language of the medieval troubadours. It is alternatively termed Occitan.

ROMANCE LANGUAGES The group of European languages descended from Latin and including Italian, Spanish, French.

SANSKRIT Among the oldest known Indo-European languages. It is a scholarly language of India dating back to the second millennium BCE.

VULGAR LATIN The language of everyday communication spoken by the ordinary people throughout the Roman Empire.

FURTHER READING
& SOURCES

Ackroyd, Peter. *Chaucer.* Vintage, London, 2005.

Arthur, Ross G. *English–Old Norse Dictionary.* Linguistics Series, Parentheses Publications, Cambridge Ontario, 2002, www.yorku.ca/in par/language/English-Old Norse. pdf.

Ayto, John. *Dictionary of Word Origins.* Bloomsbury, London, 1990.

Bryson, Bill. *Mother Tongue: The English Language.* Penguin, London, 1991.

Clark Hall, John R., and Herbert D. Meritt. *A Concise Anglo-Saxon Dictionary.* 4th edn. Cambridge University Press, Cambridge, 1960.

Cohen, J.M. and M.J. *The Penguin Dictionary of Quotations.* Penguin, Harmondsworth, 1962.

Crystal, David. *The Cambridge Encyclopedia of the English Language.* Cambridge University Press, Cambridge, 1995.

Harper, Douglas. *On-line Etymological Dictionary,* 2001, www. etymonline.com/bio.php.

Hawkins, Joyce M. (ed.). *The Oxford Reference Dictionary.* Oxford University Press, Oxford, 1991.

Hyman, Robin. *A Dictionary of Famous Quotations.* Pan, London, 1973.

Jones, Terry. *Medieval Lives.* BBC Books, London, 2005.

Lacey, Robert, and Danny Danziger. *The year 1000*. Little, Brown, London, 1999.

Lewis, Henry (ed.). *Welsh Dictionary*. Collins-Spurrell, London and Glasgow, 1962.

Liddell, Henry George, and Robert Scott. *Greek–English Lexicon*. Clarendon Press, Oxford, 1963 [1864].

Mortimer, Ian. *The Traveller's Guide to Medieval England*. Vintage Books, London, 2009.

Porter, Roy. *English Society in the 18th Century*. Penguin, London, 1991.

Ridley, Jasper. *The Tudor Age*. Robinson, London, 2002.

Simpson, D.P. *Cassell's New Latin–English, English–Latin Dictionary*. Cassell, London, 1959.

Shipley, Joseph T. *The Origins of English Words*. Johns Hopkins University Press, Baltimore MD, 1984.

Sweet, Henry. *The Student's Dictionary of Anglo-Saxon*. Clarendon Press, Oxford, 1897, https/archive.org/ details/ studentsdictionaroosweerich.

The Concise Oxford Dictionary of Quotations. Guild Publishing, London, 1990.

Thompson, Della (ed.). *The Concise Oxford Dictionary*. 9th edn. Oxford University Press, Oxford, 1995.

Tulloch, Alexander. *Word Routes: Journeys through Etymology*. Peter Owen, London, 2005.

Tulloch, Alexander. *It's All Greek: Borrowed Words and their Histories* Bodleian Library, Oxford, 2019.

INDEX OF JOBS